DATE DUE			

European
Philosophy
Today

European Philosophy Today

EDITED BY GEORGE L. KLINE

PREFACE BY MAX H. FISCH

Quadrangle Books

CHICAGO

1965

Library of Congress Catalog Card Number: 64-14136

Manufactured in the United States of America

PREFACE

This book grew out of a session on European philosophy at the meeting of the Western Division of the American Philosophical Association in 1961. The papers provoked vigorous discussion from the floor, which continued in informal groups after the session. Many participants in the discussion expressed the hope that the papers would appear together in print. I presided at that session, and thus I have the honor of introducing the papers here. My colleagues and I are grateful to Professors José Ferrater Mora and J. Glenn Gray for joining us to make a volume more representative than it was possible for the session to be.

Of the claims of Heidegger and Sartre to be considered in a volume of this scope there will be no question. The only surprise will be that, while keeping the focus on what is central in their work, Gray and Eugene F. Kaelin have been able to say so much that is both fresh and illuminating. On the other hand, the names of Kołakowski, Lombardi, and Zubiri may be new to many of our readers.

They will agree at once, however, that Eastern Europe had to be represented, and, on reflection, that it could be represented only by some form of revisionism. After reading George L. Kline's paper, they will also agree, I think, that the choice of Kołakowski was a good one. Developments still quite recent as we go to press have brought home to us the importance of political revisionism and will lend topical interest to Kline's discussion of the distinction between political and philosophical revisionism, and to his account of Kołakowski as an example of the latter.

No contemporary Italian philosopher is read and studied outside of Italy to the extent that Croce was, or even Gentile, before the Second World War; and no contemporary Spanish philosopher speaks to Europe, or even to Latin America, as Ortega y Gasset did before the Spanish Civil War. But both countries are represented by significant contemporary thinkers.

In the case of Italy, Henry S. Harris finds a worthy representative in Franco Lombardi, who thinks at least in European terms, who looks to a possible world community, and whose outlook has been reached by certain stages in the general movement of modern European philosophy; more particularly, by way of Kant, Hegel, Kierkegaard, Feuerbach, Marx, Croce, and Gentile. Harris seems, more than the authors of the other papers, to be in dialogue with the philosopher whose work he discusses—for example, with respect to the interpretation of Hegel and of Gentile.

In the first and shortest of the papers, Ferrater Mora takes us with admirable ease and economy to the center of Zubiri's philosophy, and then points to a problem there which Ferrater Mora has sought to resolve in his own philosophy. Readers lacking Spanish will be left hoping that both Zubiri's and

Ferrater Mora's works will soon be available in English translation.

During a week in Madrid in the spring of 1953, I called on the Zubiris at their apartment one day, and later attended one of the private subscription lectures which Zubiri was then giving. The audience was large. It included some members of the governmental bureaucracy, but more obviously it included leaders in the sciences and the professions. Some of them I knew as men of international eminence, in frequent communication with their colleagues abroad, both in Europe and in the Americas. One of them told me that attending Zubiri's course was not merely a high intellectual exercise and discipline but a weekly confession and penance; for they had all made their compromises with the regime, and, after sitting for an evening at the feet of the uncompromising philosopher, they went away shriven.

Zubiri himself, however, seemed neither to be the voice of any community nor to address himself to any; he was simply one man thinking. He was thinking, to be sure, in a tradition; and he seemed at times to be carrying on "a dialogue with Aristotle," or with one or another of a select few of Aristotle's heirs. But he seemed not to be in dialogue with any living philosopher, in Spain or elsewhere. I was assured, and did not doubt, that Zubiri's lectures were the best that Spain had then to offer in philosophy. Certainly the lecture I heard was of a very high order indeed. So I was confirmed in an impression previously formed, that Spain was an aggravated case of the provincialism afflicting philosophy everywhere.

Each of the five essays, taken by itself, is informing, illuminating, and provocative of philosophic reflection; and that is enough to justify the volume in which they appear together. But, reading the volume through, and bearing in mind the present philosophic scene in any English-speaking country, we may be led to some further reflections about the condition and prospects of philosophy in the world at large. For each of our five essayists, in his other publications as well as in this volume, has in effect been protesting against the provincialism of philosophy in our time, and has been doing what in him lies to create, or to revive, a community that shall include at least the English-speaking and the continental European peoples.

We can scarcely imagine what such a community would be like, for there does not even exist an English-speaking community on the one hand, nor, as these essays make evident, a continental European community on the other. But we can perhaps imagine a continental community that should include, say, three or four if not all five of the philosophers here studied; and an English-speaking community that should include one or more of the kinds of analysis now practiced, say, at Oxford, Harvard, Princeton, and Cornell. When we try to imagine these two communities, however, it is difficult to determine what positive characteristics they would have in common. It seems probable they would share three negative characteristics. Neither would take much notice of the other. Neither would take much notice of any non-Western philosophic tradition. And neither (except perhaps for its mathematical logicians) would be a part of a larger intellectual community including science.

It is not that continental European thinkers are incapable of the kinds of analysis now flourishing in English-speaking countries. There are many continental thinkers who not only admire but practice one or another of them. But these thinkers are to be found chiefly in the Scandinavian countries, in Finland, or in the Netherlands; they tend to write in English rather than in their native languages; and so they gravitate into the incipient English-speaking community. For that reason they have not been represented in this volume.

A world mathematical, scientific, and technological community, or a near approach to one, already exists, and a world community of literature and of the arts may be in the making, with films, perhaps, rather than books as its chief means of communication. If there is to be a world community of culture, it would seem that it will be created by scientists, engineers, and artists, and that there will be nothing left for philosophers but to make themselves at home—or not at home —in a world they have had no part in making.

Unless . . . —but I shall not anticipate the reader's further reflections. May he find the papers that follow as valuable as I have found them!

MAX H. FISCH

CONTENTS

European
Philosophy
Today

JOSÉ FERRATER MORA
The Philosophy of
Xavier Zubiri*

Xavier Zubiri (born 1898) is sometimes said to be Spain's most
important philosophic figure, standing immediately below—
some would say above—Ortega y Gasset. I shall not take a
position on this question, for the reason, among others, that
I do not believe that there is anyone in any country who can
properly be called "that country's most important philosophic
figure." But I do believe that Zubiri is a distinguished philosopher whose thought deserves as careful attention as that of the
better known European philosophers of the present day.

Unfortunately, I cannot undertake an adequate exposition,
much less a pertinent criticism, of Zubiri's thought. But, in the
hope of mitigating its neglect in the non-Spanish-speaking
world—both among philosophers and among persons interested

* Translated from the Spanish manuscript by George L. Kline.

15

in philosophy—I shall here give a sample of Zubiri's philosophy, discussing in relative detail one of the "permanent problems of philosophy" which he has treated most fully, namely, the problem of individuality and the individual.

Before attacking this problem, however, it will be appropriate to point out, even though sketchily, certain general features of Zubiri's thought.

A collection of Zubiri's essays was published in 1941 under the title, *Nature, History, God* (*Naturaleza, Historia, Dios*). Although certain of the fundamental ideas which were later worked out by the author were outlined in these studies, they did not appear in a mature and adequately developed form until 1962. Between 1941 and 1962 Zubiri published nothing. He limited himself to making certain of his philosophic ideas known through a series of "private lecture courses" given in Madrid, beginning in 1945, including an annual course on such themes as "Body and Soul," "God," and "Foundations of the Sciences." Some of the regular auditors of these lectures outlined Zubiri's philosophic contributions in summaries and commentaries which appeared in learned journals and especially in the volume entitled, *Homage to Xavier Zubiri* (*Homenaje a Xavier Zubiri*), 1956.

Toward the end of 1962 Zubiri published his second book, *On Essence* (*Sobre la esencia*). This was only the first of a series of "Philosophical Studies" and as such cannot be taken to represent Zubiri's finished philosophy. Certain of the fundamental themes which Zubiri elaborated in his lectures—for example: the problem of freedom, the nature of intelligence, the reality of man—are only briefly sketched in this book. However, although it is only the first of a series, this book is probably more fundamental than any which follow it in at least one respect: it offers us a "first philosophy," a "metaphysics of this world" prior both to any "second philosophy" and to any study of a possible "reality beyond this world." This book thus may be considered an exposition of the philosophical foundations of the author's thought.

Even if we reduce Zubiri's philosophic thought to its essentials, we will not find it easy to present the position which he develops in *Sobre la esencia* even in broad outline. There are two reasons for this difficulty.

The first reason is that *Sobre la esencia* is a compact book, rigorously systematic in nature—quite the opposite of what Kant called "a philosophic rhapsody." It contains the foundations of a system different from any of the "traditional" ones, or at least different from those systems in which parts of the system correspond to the various philosophic disciplines. One cannot say that Zubiri's philosophic thought contains, for example, "a logic," "a theory of knowledge," "an ethics," "a metaphysics," etc. But Zubiri's theses and arguments are systematic in the sense of being rigorously interlocked: no one of them can be omitted without a serious loss of comprehensibility of the others.

The second reason is that Zubiri has for some time been introducing a philosophic terminology which requires explanation. Some of the new terms which he has introduced are semantically linked to traditional terms—for example, "substantive" ("sustantivo") and "substantivity" ("sustantividad") in contrast to "substantial" ("sustancial") and "substantiality" ("sustancialidad"); "objectual" ("objetual") and "objectuality" ("objetualidad"), in contrast to "objective" ("objetivo") and "objectivity" ("objetividad"). But this does not make it any easier to understand his new terms; rather it makes it more difficult, because there is the danger of confusing the meaning of the "derived" term with that of the "original" term. Certain of the other new terms introduced by Zubiri are old words used in a new sense—for example, "solidity" ("solidez"), "endure" ("estar siendo"), "on its own" ("de suyo"), and of course "essence" ("esencia"), "existence" ("existencia"), "reality" ("realidad"), "being" ("ser"). Some of his new terms are in current philosophic use, but they appear in *Sobre la esencia* with quite different meanings. This is the case, for example, with the words "constitutive" ("constitutivo") and "constitutional" ("constitucional").

I thus find myself constrained to offer a summary description of certain of the fundamental features of Zubiri's philosophy, without taking into account either its systematic structure or its special vocabulary. With these limitations in mind, I shall single out the following points:

(1) To begin with, the book's title, *Sobre la esencia*, is itself somewhat misleading. What Zubiri means by "essence" is not any specific or generic, logical or metaphysical, essence, but rather the "essence of the real" or, if one prefers, "the real as essence." The essence in question is examined metaphysically, but it is not something metaphysical; rather it is "physical," in the sense which the predicate "is physical" has when it approaches, and even becomes identical with, the sense of the predicate "is real."

Zubiri's "physical essence" or "real essence" thus differs, both really and conceptually, from the idea of essence adopted by several authors whom Zubiri considers in some detail: essence as the "ideal unit of meaning" (Husserl); essence as "formal concept" (Hegel); essence as "objective concept" (Leibniz); essence as "real correlate of the definition" (Aristotle). This does not mean that Zubiri fails to make use of the important suggestions and contributions of his predecessors. A list of the philosophers whom one might suspect of having significantly influenced Zubiri would include those just mentioned, especially Aristotle, as well as others whose names appear throughout the book—the Scholastics in general, Duns Scotus and Suárez in particular; and at least two others who are closer in time than any of those hitherto mentioned: Heidegger, whom Zubiri discusses in order to refute the thesis that being is prior to reality, and Ortega y Gasset, whom, for reasons which it would be tedious to state in detail, he does not mention at all.

Thus, the doctrine expounded in *Sobre la esencia* is by no means a "foreign body" in the history of philosophy. However, Zubiri makes use of the doctrines of his predecessors as points of departure, or points of support, rather than as elements from which to construct his own doctrine in a more or less eclectic way.

(2) If "essence" is understood provisionally in the proposed sense, we can formulate Zubiri's three central questions as follows: (a) what is it that is "essentiable" ("lo esenciable"); (b) what realities are "essentiated" ("esenciadas"); (c) of what does essence consist?

(3) The answer to the first two questions is relatively simple. The "essentiable" is the "physical," that is to say, "real things." Essentiated realities are those which must have certain features (*notas*) if they are to be constituted as realities. These features, or characteristics, are not "necessary" in the sense that either they or the corresponding thing necessarily exists, but they *are* "necessary" in the sense that without them the thing in question would not be. These features, moreover, must belong to the thing as a real thing subsisting for itself, and not as a thing which occasionally functions in one way or another. The features of the reality "gold" are necessary to the being of such a reality. That a gold object should serve to reflect light is external to the reality "gold." What is essentiated in gold (let us formulate the point tautologically for the moment) is *being golden*, but not, for example, *reflecting*.

(4) The answer to the third question is a long one. Strictly speaking such an answer would include the main elements of Zubiri's "first philosophy." In order to answer this question we must elucidate the following themes, among others: (a) of what does essence consist; (b) which features are essential; (c) of what does the essential unity consist; (d) in what way, or ways, does essence refer not only to the real, but also to the transcendental, order?

(5) Let us now confine ourselves, without necessarily following the order just indicated, to clarifying certain points about essence. It should be emphasized that the essence of which Zubiri speaks is not a more or less msyterious reality situated "beyond the real thing"; the essence is the thing itself, insofar as it is *such* a thing and insofar as it is *real*. An essence is thus the essence of what Zubiri calls a "substantive reality." A *substantive* reality differs from a *substantial* reality in that, whereas the latter is, metaphysically speaking, "a subject of inherence" and, logically speaking, "a subject of predication," the former is simply a system of features which "close off" the thing and render it "substantive." The features referred to constitute the thing as a substantive unity. In order to understand, even if imperfectly, the difference between *substantial* reality, or *substantiality*, and *substantive* reality, or *substantivity*, we may offer the following examples: An organic body is a substantive reality composed of substantial realities (its physico-chemical elements), which might formerly have been substantive, but which lost their substantivity when they entered into another system. This indicates that, although in many cases a substantive reality may at the same time be substantial, not all substantivities are substantialities, and vice versa. Thus there may be insubstantial substances—realities which are defective in what Zubiri calls "the constitutional order." In other words, the essence is the thing itself as substantive reality, that is to say, as a reality which is adequate in a given constitutional order.

(6) Essence thus has an individual, entitative character; it is not a "logical element" or a "metaphysical foundation" of reality. This means that the reality in question is always an individual entity, whether it is merely singular or is fully individual. Essence constitutes the entity as individual. Hence, essence is not definable in the way that generic and specific essences are. Instead of the process called "definition," Zubiri proposes a

device called "essential proposition"—something which is always "open" to possible new essential features.

(7) This conception of essence presupposes a certain conception of the language in which one speaks, or may speak, about essence. This point is particularly important but also particularly difficult, and we cannot linger over it here. We shall limit ourselves to noting that Zubiri develops a conception of the *logos* that is different from those conceptions which may be subsumed under expressions like "defining *logos*" (or simply "definition"), "descriptive *logos*" (or simply "description"), etc. The *logos*, or linguistic structure, insofar as it is relative to the real, is a *logos* based on a mode of language which Zubiri calls "language as construct" (an example is Hebrew). The "construct state" of language is a morphological device by means of which, in the author's words, "the real is conceptualized as a unitary system of things, the latter being constructed one after the other, and forming a whole among themselves." [1] The "construct state" is thus distinct from that state of language in which either noun declension or the prepositional form prevails (an example is Greek).

(8) It would be interesting now to show how essence, which has heretofore been understood as the essence of the real thing as *such* a thing (essence as "suchness" [*talidad*]) can be understood as an essence referring to a transcendental structure (essence as "reality" pure and simple). But that would increase the difficulties which we have confronted in touching on the points thus far presented to such an extent as to make our task truly impossible. This is regrettable because, in his investigation of the transcendental order, Zubiri has some very suggestive things to say not only about the Scholastics but also and especially about Heidegger. Against the Scholastics, Zubiri argues that "world" is a transcendental term. Against Heidegger, he argues that "being is not a species of supreme character in-

1. Xavier Zubiri, *Sobre la esencia* (Madrid, 1962), p. 355.

volving the whole of what is real": "real things," he adds, "'are,' but Being does not have substantivity." [2]

(9) It would be no less interesting and no less philosophical to examine critically at least a few of Zubiri's major theses. But it would not be possible unless the reader were already familiar with them. Since these are recent theses (or since their systematic formation is recent) and since it is very likely that they will be less well known to the non-Spanish reader than those of certain other contemporary authors, it has seemed to us that we could contribute something to the volume for which these pages are intended by simply familiarizing the reader with the most essential of them. Assuming that we have achieved this end, we shall now proceed to examine in somewhat greater detail one theme of Zubiri's philosophy: the theme of the structure of individuality and the individual as this theme is set forth in *Sobre la esencia*, ch. 8, sec. 3.

Although the theme of individuality and the individual is not isolated from other themes, it is relatively isolable, especially if, in addition to the passage cited, we keep in mind what the author says in ch. 9, sec. 1, and in the same chapter sec. 2, art. 2. We shall now consider simply what the individual is for Zubiri; in order not to complicate matters excessively, we shall neglect a distinction which in other respects would be important: the distinction between "singularity" and "strict individuality" or, alternatively, between the meaning of the predicate "is singular" and the meaning of the predicate "is (strictly) individual." For our purposes it will be enough to consider only "the individual."

Zubiri begins by reversing a tendency which philosophers have stubbornly exhibited: that of making the individual a conceptual "contraction" of the species. Not only is the individual not a "contraction" of the species; on the contrary, what we

2. *Ibid.*, p. 436.

call a "species" can be understood as an "expansion" of the individual. This seems to lead to a serious difficulty which is found not at the level of reality itself but at the level of the language in which we discuss reality. Indeed, if the individual is not a contraction of the species, it seems that we will not even be able to speak of the individual, since "to speak of," in the sense which concerns us here, is "to conceptualize"; and no conceptualization seems feasible unless we introduce into our language predicates which as such are "universal"— either specific or generic.

It may be said that this difficulty is fictitious, because we can perfectly well renounce all intention of "conceptualizing," considering the latter a distortion of reality. In such a case we would replace concepts with other modes of understanding. One—but only one—of them is "intuition." Indeed, in addition to claiming that we can intuit reality as individual reality, we may claim to be able to "manipulate" it. If we refuse to be "rationalists," we can be not only "intuitionists," but also pragmatists, operationalists, etc. However, Zubiri continues to be a "rationalist," if by "rationalism" we now understand the assumption that the real is conceptualizable. However, the problem remains: the individual is not a "contraction" of the species, but this does not make it any less conceptualizable. To admit that the whole of reality is individual is not the same thing as refusing to speak of the individual, or of its individuality, by means of concepts.

It may be alleged that there is nothing fundamentally new in the inversion which Zubiri has carried out and that—as indeed Zubiri himself notes—Aristotle had a glimpse of the possibility of seeing the individual in a way distinct from that which was habitual in much of the philosophic tradition. This is not surprising. There are good reasons—although not always those which people have been accustomed to bring forward— for regarding Aristotle as *philosophus, the* philosopher. But Aristotle is in a class by himself: he is a philosopher who has touched upon truths of great scope but has then withdrawn from them. Whether this Aristotelian withdrawal had as one of its causes what may be called a "Platonic obsession" is a point which cannot be developed in four words—or in four thousand. But one thing is certain: Aristotle habitually "thinks twice," and his second thought—which is the one that has customarily exercised the greater influence—is almost always inferior.

He has tended to superimpose upon his first thought an interpretation that does not correspond to his original way of seeing things. Thus it could be said that on this central point Zubiri restores Aristotle's "true position." But apart from the fact that this would not mean very much, it would also be inaccurate, first, because there is no such thing as a philosopher's "true position"; second, because even if there were such a thing, this would not mean that Zubiri is "more Aristotelian than Aristotle." Zubiri's ideas about the individual are not Aristotelian except to the extent that his thought is in large measure "a dialogue with Aristotle" (and of course with Hegel, Kant, Scholasticism, etc., as well).

For reasons similar to those already given, it is not legitimate to say that the position which Zuburi takes on the present problem is a reaffirmation of a certain tradition according to which—as is the case in Suárez—it is recognized that individuals have features which are essential to them as individuals. This is clearly true and says a good deal in Suárez's favor. But it is one thing to recognize the existence of the "individual physical essence" and another and quite different thing to work out a theory about it. Indeed, from the fact that something is individual *in* itself we cannot conclude that it is individual *for* itself. The former might very well be the case, and yet the latter might not follow. To show that the latter is admissible and even indispensable, Zubiri treats the problem of the individual—and that of the essence to the degree that it discharges, or is thought to discharge, a "structuring function" ("funcion estructurante")—by the method of "non-specification" and "non-contraction."

But what happens when we decide not to restrict individuality by means of operations like specification, contraction, and differentiation?

(1) Zubiri alleges that individuation is not a principle or a series of principles; it is an "integral aspect of reality" ("momento de la realidad"). Therefore, no principle of individuation is required in order for something to be an individual, or in order to explain that something is an individual. This assertion seems similar to Leibniz's (the Leibniz of the "Fourth Letter" to Clarke or of bk. 2, ch. 27, of the *Nouveaux Essais*, not the Leibniz of the *Confessio philosophi*). For Leibniz spoke of the "principle of individuation," but he maintained that such a principle is "an internal principle of distinction," that is to say, that the internal differences were grounded in "intrinsic denominations." This also seems similar to the assertion that we find in Suárez' fifth *Disputatio* (sec. 6, art. 1), where he formally declares that no other principle of individuation is required beyond the being (or the intrinsic principles of which such being is made up) of the individual in question. Suárez reminds us that this claim—which he calls *clarissima*—had already been made by Aureol, Durand de Saint-Pourçain, and others.

Although there may be elements of Leibnizianism and especially of Suarezism in Zubiri, this is not enough to permit us to identify the two positions. On the one hand, both Leibniz and Suárez spoke of substances and not of substantivities (see above). In contrast, the individual as treated here is primarily a substantive reality, that is to say, a system of essential features and not, or not necessarily, a substantial reality, that is, a subject of predicates. On the other hand, and most importantly, in both Leibniz and Suárez the intrinsic character of the individual thing is constituted, in the final analysis, by a conjunction of "properties" and thus, from the logical point of view, of "predications."

This is particularly clear in Leibniz. In the contrary case it would be impossible to understand the meaning and function of the Principle of the Identity of Indiscernibles. What is discernible or not discernible is properties—properties of a substance. These properties may, if one wishes, be identified with "states," but this does not fundamentally change Leibniz's position on this point. Properties or "states" are equally expressible, and uniquely expressible, in extensional terms. The entities in question arc said to be identical when and only when they have the same extensional properties. Expressed in the language of logic, Leibniz's metaphysics exhibits the "non-individual" foundation of individuality.

(2) The rejection of the predicative foundation of individuality is not mitigated by recurring to some other foundation, such as classes. In the last analysis, classes and properties are parallel. The situation is not helped by an appeal to relations. Without doubt, relational language is capable of expressing equations (inequalities as well as equalities). But in equations individualities are dissolved, metaphysically speaking, into "lattices of relations." In this case we proceed not by differentiation, but by "intersection." However, the result is practically the same. In every case we abstract from individuality as something "constituted" and "structured."

We should recognize that there are interesting analogies between systems of relations and what Zubiri calls "systems of features." But there are also differences which are no less interesting. To begin with, the individual is primarily and *formaliter* entitative rather than relational: every relation which is essential in character is a relational system *of* the individual entity. Next, and most importantly, the constitutive features of the individual are "features-of" (where to be a feature is equivalent to being the entity) and not simply "features of" (where the features are simply possible properties of the entity). In other words, the system of essential features really structures the individual, that is, constitutes it as *this* individual. The essential features are real aspects and not parts of the individual.

In some sense, Zubiri's doctrine of the real constitution of the individual through its essential features presupposes a "theory of parts and wholes" of which we have some interesting examples in contemporary philosophy—e.g., Leśniewski's "mereology" and the "theory of parts and wholes" in Husserl's *Logische Untersuchungen*. But in Leśniewski's mereology such features—or that which exercises their function—are limited to the structuring of singularities, and in Husserl's "theory of parts and wholes" there is an emphasis upon only such aspects as "dependence" and "non-dependence." Furthermore, Husserl declares in the end that essences are not realities but "ideal units of meaning."

(3) From what has been said, it may be seen that the doctrine of individuality proposed by Zubiri amounts to an admission that individuals differ essentially among themselves. Essence as "real essence" is, in sum, "individual essence." But this does not mean that each individual differs from others by virtue of a "substantial form" which is proper to it. This cannot be the case for several of the reasons already alluded to; among others because individuals are not, strictly speaking, substances. But in addition, and most importantly, the essential difference between individuals is grounded in a "real mode" and not in a "quidditative mode," however individual the latter may be. Neither quiddity nor form "constitutes" the real individual: only reality itself, as a system of essential features, constitutes it and, of course, also structures it.

Thus we might possibly conclude that the real world of which Zubiri speaks is simply "a world of individuals," similar to the world which some nominalists have described. But the matter is not so simple. To begin with, Zubiri does not think that "anything whatever" is an individual. Strictly speaking, there are very few things in the world which appear to be individual. Therefore, after having insisted on the individual—or more or less fully individual—character of the real thing, Zubiri seems to take a step backward, admitting that although only the individual is real—or "physically real"—there are very few realities which are individuals *stricto sensu*.

(4) I believe that some of the most serious difficulties which Zubiri's philosophic thought confronts are located at this point. Certain of these difficulties are due to the fact that Zubiri has excessively emphasized the independent entitative character of the "real thing." This has forced him to stress the individual nature, or the nature which in principle is individual, of the real thing. But at the same time he has had to recognize that real things are less "closed off" by their essential features than would appear at first sight. He has gone so far as to admit that only the material cosmos as a whole has substantivity—which means, let us not forget, substantive *reality*.

Thus a conflict has been generated from which one could perhaps escape by admitting that the concept of individuality is a limiting concept, and that individuality, like reality, is something essentially defective—metaphysically defective.[3] This means that it is not defective relative to the sufficiency or completeness of some other reality, but defective in itself. The being of reality might very well consist in never coming to be fully. But this is a theme which would take a long time to be developed and which in any case cannot be treated here.

3. I have outlined this conception of individuality in a forthcoming book, *Being and Death*, my own translation of *El ser y la muerte* (Madrid, 1962). The underlying ontology is being developed in my work-in-progress, *Being and Meaning (El ser y el sentido)*.

BIBLIOGRAPHY OF THE PRINCIPAL WRITINGS OF XAVIER ZUBIRI

Ensayo de una teoría fenomenológica del juicio (doctoral dissertation), 1923.

Naturaleza, Historia, Dios, fourth edition, Madrid, 1959. Original edition: 1941.

Sobre la esencia (Estudios Filosóficos, I), Madrid, 1962.

Cinco lecciones de filosofía, Madrid, 1963. (On Aristotle, Kant, Comte, Bergson, Husserl, Dilthey, and Heidegger.)

"El hombre, realidad personal," *Revista de Occidente* (Madrid), Año 1, seg. ép. (1963), pp. 5-29.

"El origen del hombre," *Revista de Occidente,* Año 2, seg. ép. (1964), pp. 146-173.

J. GLENN GRAY
The New Image of Man in Martin Heidegger's Philosophy

I

Every philosopher of note, according to Martin Heidegger, thinks a single great idea. His mission in life is to bring forth this idea in all possible nuances and to illuminate the shadows, that is, the unthought elements even in the most familiar concept. For Heidegger the single idea is Being. So persistently does he attempt to think about the nature of Being that the Germans joke about Heidegger's *Wacht am Sein.* The soldier's watch on the Rhine has at length given place to the philosopher's watch over Being!

Yet what a thinker intends and what he accomplishes are frequently quite different. A generation ago Theodor Haering chose a happy title for his book on Hegel when he called it: *Hegel: Sein Wollen und sein Werk.* I want to suggest in this essay that the genuine originality in Heidegger's philosophy lies as much in his interpretation of human nature as in his attempts to clarify the meaning of Being.

A problem that has been central for Heidegger throughout his life is the way man relates himself to his world; to his own past, present, and future, to the utensils and implements of his everyday life, to the things and creatures of Nature, to his fellow human beings, and to the complex of all of these. Kant's fourth question: What is man? has been Heidegger's question, too, though his answer is a different one. Many of his essays and lectures of the last three decades have been concerned with the plight of contemporary man in alienation from his world, an alienation occasioned by the growth of a technological mentality and by unfortunate philosophical traditions. Though Heidegger's declared intention has been to think Being truly, his accomplishment has been to elucidate the kind of being, namely the human being, who does that thinking. Man is a being, in his very suggestive definition, who is concerned about his own being. And Heidegger's attempts to illuminate the kind of being man has, or rather is, has resulted in a significant change in the images of man to which Western tradition has become accustomed.

The question of the nature of man is, however, for him a philosophical question, not a psychological, moral, or social one. Heidegger is not interested in the problems of the recent and fashionable philosophical anthropology. I think it necessary to take seriously his protests that his writings have been basically misunderstood by friends and enemies alike. He is primarily interested in the phenomenon of man, not as an historical species nor as a social, political or biological creature, but as an appearance in the history of Being. His basic point is that man cannot be understood apart from his relation to Being itself, to which he belongs and whose essence he recurrently seeks to understand.

Heidegger's mission is to awaken man's memory of Being as such. Once man remembers his origin aright, he will presumably seek to relate his way of being to that of which it is a small part. Hence Heidegger's insistence on the priority of ontology in the search for the human essence. His questioning is directed toward understanding man in the perspective of Being, not the reverse of this, which he thinks has been a fundamental mistake of our philosophical tradition, that is, trying to understand Being by investigating the human being.

In what follows it is necessary to hold this in mind. We do not understand human beings by abstracting their essence from the world to which they belong, the world conceived either in terms of individual things or creatures or the sum total of such individual existents, which is the subject matter of metaphysics. Above all, we do not understand human nature by abstracting it from Being as such, which is the subject matter of ontology. Heidegger's case against his interpreters is that they mistake his basic endeavor by confusing metaphysics with ontology.

The three images of man in the Western tradition that are most familiar are the Christian, which defines man's essence in terms of an immortal soul whose origin and destiny are apart from the world, the Greek image of man as a rational animal, a species among other living creatures with reason added, and the modern biological image of man as a *homo faber*, an intelligent animal who has learned in the struggle for existence to fabricate and use tools. Against all three images Heidegger directs his attacks: against the Christian because it attempts to get at man's essence from a reality outside the experienced world, from a transcendent Being; against the physiological or biological image because it assimilates man to other living forms and disregards his uniqueness. But it is against the Greek image of man as an *animal rationale*, or in the Greek language a *zōon logon echon*, that he directs his main polemic. This he regards as chiefly responsible for the contemporary biological image.

This Greek conception of man, in Heidegger's view, was formulated not by the pre-Socratic philosophers nor by the poets, but by Plato and Aristotle, who are at the origin of the fundamental misunderstanding of human nature which has prevailed ever since, for even the Christian interpretation has taken over essential aspects of their conception of the rational animal. On the other hand, Heraclitus and Parmenides grasped man's nature more fundamentally than did their more renowned successors, and so did Sophocles as well as a few modern poets, especially Hölderlin.

To understand man as an animal with reason is correct in a formal or logical sense, Heidegger asserts, but it misses the deeper truth about man as a project of Being, or *physis*, as the pre-Socratics grasped Being. The mistaken view places man at the top of a hierarchy of other forms of life, like them except with reason added. In such fashion Western metaphysics has tried to grasp man's essence as an amalgam of animality and rationality. Heidegger is inclined to ascribe to this way of thinking most of the confusion and radical error of philosophical thought. For metaphysics is unable to bridge the dichotomy between subject and object. It regards this distinction as self-evident and the starting point for analysis of the world and of man, thus making impossible any union of the human way of being with Being as such. Metaphysics is habituated to thinking in representational ways and defining truth as the adequate correspondence between the idea in our minds and the object of that idea in the objective world. This leads, in Heidegger's opinion, to the contemporary curse of subjectivism in metaphysics as well as to its opposite, but related, tendency, to "the absolute objectivization of everything." [1] In both cases the mistake is made, at the starting point, of failing to grasp the human essence as part and parcel of the world in which it appears.

This fundamental alienation of man from his sources, his home and true dwelling place, is Heidegger's deepest persuasion

1. "Letter on Humanism," tr. by Edgar Lohner, in *Philosophy in the Twentieth Century*, ed. by W. Barrett and H. D. Aiken (New York, 1962), II, 273.

about the modern world. This persuasion gives the poignant edge to many of his later lectures and essays. At the philosophical level it is responsible for his life-long attempt to create a fundamental ontology that will bridge the chasm between the being of man and that vast realm of Being toward which he is directed.

It should not be thought that Heidegger blames Plato and Aristotle for this wrong turning in the history of Western philosophy. That they thought the way they did is determined by the history of Being itself, which somehow governs its own development. Man was fated to this falling away from his true relation to Being and to the pursuit of this false path until it reached its conclusion, which Heidegger believes took place in modern times in the philosophies of Hegel and Nietzsche. "The history of Being sustains and determines every *condition et situation humaine*." [2]

Had it not been for this wrong turning, the modern image of man as a technical animal and the development of modern science and technology would have been unthinkable. In his dislike for these contemporary developments and his preference for the primordial sources of Western philosophical thinking, Heidegger is sometimes believed to be advocating a return to pre-Socratic philosophy as the only hope for the future. But he has made it clear in a recent (1957) essay entitled "The Onto-theological Nature of Metaphysics" that he has taken a step back in the history of thought in order to make a leap forward into Being. The pre-Socratics are a means to the end of a new union of man with Being. They represent a way to rethink the history of metaphysics, which has finally worked out its consequences and revealed its dangers for our day. Past philosophies, in short, are not to be condemned but reflected upon and made use of for what they can contribute to our perilous age, threatened philosophically by forgetfulness of Being and loss of truth.

It is likewise important to remember that Heidegger is not

2. *Ibid.*, p. 271.

condemning, at least most of the time and in his more recent writings, the religious, the rational, and the biological images of man. In some fashion they have their place and their rightness in the history of Being; they are trying to get at certain features of the human phenomenon. The existential image that he is bringing forth is a kind of fulfillment of previous attempts to conceive human nature truly.

II

What are the main features of this existential image of man as seen by Heidegger? A reply must take into account that these features have been slowly evolved by him throughout a lifetime of reflection which is still in process. I think it is evident that they have undergone considerable filling out, surely, too, some alteration in the course of his publications from *Being and Time* in 1927, *Introduction to Metaphysics*, 1935, the "Letter on Humanism," 1947 to *Vorträge und Aufsätze* in 1954. It is with these works that I shall be concerned in the rest of this essay.

In his first major publication, *Being and Time*, Heidegger went to great lengths to emphasize that man's essence is inseparable from the world in which he comes to consciousness. It is impossible to investigate the human kind of being in isolation from its environment, from speech and language, from "the things at hand," from the objects and creatures present in Nature, and from other human beings. Man is not human at all when conceived as a separate or separable entity, either as an individual or a species. He is essentially a Being-with-others and in the midst-of-things. I reiterate this central point of Heidegger's, for it separates him most sharply from Kierkegaard and Sartre, existentialists who have had the greater impact on American thought.

The human being, then is a being in a world which is an integral part of his being. "World," as Heidegger uses the term, does not stand for an entity; it is not the equivalent of the biologist's term "environment." For him, world includes not only the factual, sensuous surroundings, but the vast realm of possibilities as well. For the individual the world includes the past, present and future of a creation in process. World is both what objectively exists independent of man, in infinitely variegated forms, and the inner, imagined and imaginary state of mind of every single consciousness. And these two realms are not separated but unified—unified at least for the individual who is truly himself and hence in direct contact with the real world. World is, too, what the pre-Socratics called *physis*, the term that has always come closest to Heidegger's "Being."

This emphasis of Heidegger's signifies what Walter Schulz has called "a desubstantializing of the ego." [3] Heidegger starts from a rejection of the Cartesian *res cogitans*. Man does not possess a nature already formed. On the contrary, he creates it and continues to recreate it as he responds to the things and creatures of his experience. Descartes belongs to those metaphysical thinkers who, according to Heidegger, are incapable of conceiving experience other than in a subject-object dichotomy and in a static, timeless framework.

Yet man is in the world in a basically different way from all other creatures. Hence it is a mistaking of his essence to apply the categories which philosophers such as Aristotle and Kant have used for interpreting other phenomena. Instead one must understand man in terms of existentialities which characterize him alone and which are his way of relating himself to the world. They represent the degree of his attunement or lack of attunement to Being. If our word "mood" did not possess merely emotional and psychological connotations, it could perhaps be an acceptable synonym for existentiality. The existentialities Heidegger is concerned with form the under-

---

3. Walter Schulz, "Über den philosophiegeschichtlichen Ort Martin Heideggers," in *Philosophische Rundschau,* 1 (1953-1954), 65-93, 211-233; cf. also my article, "Heidegger's Course: From Human Existence to Nature," *Journal of Philosophy,* 54 (1957), 197-207.

lying disposition or temperament which fuses reason and feeling to make us open or closed to the world we inhabit. Such disposition is neither inherent nor unchanging. Nor is it, of course, a fusion of animality and rationality, but rather a unique structure of relationships and potentialities.

The most fundamental of the existentialities which form this new image of man is Care (*Sorge*). In the key sixth chapter of the first half of *Being and Time*, entitled in the English translation, "Care as the Being of *Dasein*," Heidegger reaches the core of his analysis of the human way of being. He makes use of an ancient fable about Care, which Goethe also appropriated for the second part of *Faust*. Here it is in the translation of Macquarrie and Robinson:

> Once when "Care" was crossing a river, she saw some clay; she thoughtfully took up a piece and began to shape it. While she was meditating on what she had made, Jupiter came by. "Care" asked him to give it spirit, and this he gladly granted. But when she wanted her name to be bestowed upon it, he forbade this, and demanded that it be given his name instead. While "Care" and Jupiter were disputing, Earth arose and desired that her own name be conferred upon the creature, since she had furnished it with part of her body. They asked Saturn to be their arbiter, and he made the following decision, which seemed a just one: "Since you, Jupiter, have given its spirit, you shall receive that spirit at its death; and since you, Earth, have given its body, you shall receive its body. But since "Care" first shaped this creature, she shall possess it as long as it lives And because there is now a dispute among you as to its name, let it be called "homo," for it is made out of *humus* (earth).[4]

Though this fable represents a pre-ontological way of understanding man, it is nevertheless primordial, and this, as students of Heidegger know, gives it a most significant status. The earlier the thought, other things being equal, the more pro-

4. *Being and Time*, tr. by J. Macquarrie and E. Robinson (Oxford and New York, 1962), p. 242.

found and revealing. Heidegger calls attention to certain features of the story. Saturn, who symbolizes time, determines the primordial being of this creature, "man." He is named "homo" not in consideration of his being but in relation to that of which he consists. Man during his "temporal sojourn in the world" is dominated through and through by Care.

"Care" is a word of many connotations, in the German language even more than in English. And unlike English, the German can suggest these significations by using the word *Sorge* as a root. Heidegger takes full advantage of this. The key ambiguity of the term lies in both languages, however, in the double meaning of "care": in the denotation of "anxious effort" on the one hand and "carefulness" and "devotion" on the other. One is burdened with care when harried, worried, or grieved, and lightened by care when one cares for, takes care of, protects and cherishes loved things or persons. The word "concern" (*Besorgen* in German) has become, as everyone knows, of central importance in existentialist thought generally. Anxiety or Dread, so important for Kierkegaard and Sartre, is also an existentiality for Heidegger, but it is a subordinate structure of Care.

This double (actually multiple) meaning of *Sorge* forms the foundation for Heidegger's new image of man. Man's essence is discovered in the care or concern he takes about the kind of being he is. When he relates himself aright to the world, and to Being itself, the positive and happier denotations of Care manifest themselves. Man as a solicitous, protective, and cherishing creature appears. But when he alienates himself from his essence as a being-in-the-world and a guardian of Being as such, the negative and cheerless aspects of Care are manifest, such as anxiety, fallenness into the impersonal "they," idle curiosity, chatter, and the like.

It is, however, necessary to caution the reader once more that Heidegger conceives these existentialities as ontological, as integral parts of the structure of Being in general. They are easily interpreted in what he calls "ontic" terms, that is, psychological or anthropological categories. The point is that individuals do not consciously turn to or away from their essence in Being. Their attunement or lack of attunement Heidegger constantly regards as a kind of fate, which is not beyond human intervention but also not wholly subservient to it. In analogy to Christian grace, it must first be extended before it can be appropriated.

Near the end of the sixth chapter (on "Care as the Being of *Dasein*") in *Being and Time*, Heidegger summarizes four typical features of the human relation to Being which specify the way he conceives the structure of care as man's essence. I prefer to paraphrase the section rather than to follow the translation, which is not always a happy one. My treatment here will of necessity be brief and insufficient for any full understanding of this complex chapter, which deserves detailed study.

By virtue of his existential nature, Heidegger asserts, man stands in the truth of Being. Truth belongs both to man and to Being, if truth be properly understood in the ancient Greek sense as *alētheia*, an uncovering of that which is hidden. Man is *in* the truth insofar as he is authentically what he is, a child of Care. Hence the first and abiding characteristic of the human being is "openness as such" (*Erschlossenheit überhaupt*). Man, because he is primordially concern or care, is able to experience Being and abide in its nearness.

Secondly, and as a constitutive part of this quality of openness to the truth, the individual exists in the world in a condition of Thrownness (*Geworfenheit*). By this idea Heidegger means simply that the human way of being is discovered always in solitary individuals who are in a definite and particular world with their own private image of that world. If man as such is open to the disclosures of Being, it is only to single individuals in isolated consciousness that Being discloses itself.

A third essential characteristic of man as a creature of Care is his quality of being a project or projection (*Entwurf*). By this he means that an individual can understand human nature either in terms of the world and his fellow human beings or he can understand it by entering intimately into the potentialities of his own nature. In the second case, Heidegger reminds us, the mode of authenticity comes most powerfully into play. A kind of primordial openness is possible to one who grasps authentically his own existential being, which not only reveals him to himself but also reveals something of the truth of the larger realm of Being as such. Heidegger is further suggesting by the notion of "project" that the human being is a "sketch" of Being itself and, to those who are most genuine individuals, much of Being's own mysterious reality can be disclosed through self-understanding.

Finally, to the kind of being that man is belongs the state or quality of fallenness. Men are in the first instance, and most men always are, "lost" in their world. Though the truth of Being is open, there is, according to Heidegger, a predilection in human beings toward the condition of being absorbed into the public, impersonal, and inauthentic world. The true nature of things is constantly being covered up to man's concern and care. He must wrest from the world its truth, tear off the veil that conceals even the simplest entities, and enter into himself, his fellows, and the things and creatures of Nature more profoundly than he is wont to do, if he is to live in the truth. Alienation and lostness are the more common state; hence the general impression conveyed by *Being and Time* in its entirety is that man is almost destined to untruth and to a decadent state of life.

However, Heidegger assures his readers even in this work, and more explicitly in his later writings, that he does not believe in the fall of man in the Christian sense. The existentiality of Care that is man's essence can discover the truth of the world and remain open to continuing disclosures of the nature of things. Moreover, the affirmative qualities of care can gain control of man, even if "at first and for the most part" the negative and depressing ones are more apparent on life's surface.

III

For there is another existentiality in this structure of care with which Heidegger has been concerned throughout his career, the analysis of which, subtly changing from the earlier to the later works, brings out the extent to which human beings can find themselves at home in the world. I refer to the phenomenon of "uncanniness" which is the English translation of *Unheimlichkeit*, literally the un-homelike. In many ways this disposition in man is the most interesting of all Heidegger's analyses and his treatment of it the most revealing of his own standpoint on human nature.

In *Being and Time* the phenomenon of the uncanny is associated with anxiety, that nameless and indefinite fear which on occasion grips the individual who is lost in his world and menaced by *das Nichts*. Such a person flees into the public and impersonal realm and manages to forget the fact that he is lost. Yet this inauthentic state of being is now and then threatened by the disposition of uncanniness. Heidegger calls it a basic kind of being-in-the-world. Uncanniness pursues the human creature and is a threat to the lostness in which it has forgotten itself.[5] The ontological source of this existentiality, as Heidegger makes explicit in his major work, is the principle of individuation, the fact that human consciousness always and only appears in single individuals. It is that quality of the structure of Care which, as we have seen, Heidegger calls Thrownness. We are cast by Being itself into existence in individuated, isolated form. Anxiety arises when the individual seeks to

5. Cf. *ibid.*, p. 234.

escape from this primal aloneness and singularity, flees into the crowd and hides from his potential selfhood.

The threat of the uncanny runs like a thread through the various analyses of *Being and Time*, without ever receiving a separate treatment. Heidegger feels that it is ever-present in human existence, even in the most tranquil and familiar states of mind. The consciousness of being without a home, in the metaphorical sense of the word, can come over us at any time, exposing us to the most disturbing sort of anxiety. Uncanniness is at the root of the notion of conscience (treated in a later chapter of *Being and Time*), conscience which calls to us from the depths of our being to actualize our unique potentialities. We become anxious in our lostness and fall prey to the sense of homelessness because we have failed to realize our most intimate and authentic potentialities for relating ourselves to Being.

However, in his lectures on "An Introduction to Metaphysics," delivered in Freiburg in 1935 and first published in 1953, Heidegger analyzes the phenomenon of the uncanny in a separate and considerably altered fashion. This analysis occurs in the context of an extended discussion of Parmenides' and Heraclitus' understanding of Being and is in the nature of a long digression on Sophocles' *Antigone*, specifically on the famous first chorus of the poem, lines 332-375. According to Heidegger, Sophocles, in his poetic fashion, has, like the pre-Socratics, perceived truly in these lines the mutual bond between man and Being itself.

Incidentally, it is of interest to note that *Antigone* played a considerable role in Hegel's philosophy. Hegel called it the noblest product of the Hellenic spirit and drew from it his most important distinction between private morality and social ethics. Heidegger in a different way discovers Sophocles in this drama to be peculiarly aware of the phenomenon of the uncanny as that which is basic to man's nature.

Limitations of space prohibit my citing the whole passage, but the first two lines are of chief concern in Heidegger's treatment. They stand in his translation:

Vielfältig das Unheimliche, nichts doch
über den Menschen hinaus Unheimlicheres ragend sich regt.[6]

which his translator, Ralph Manheim renders:

There is much that is strange, but nothing that surpasses man in strangeness.[7]

Manheim chooses to translate Heidegger's *Unheimliche* with the word "strange," rather than "uncanny." The Greek word is *deinon* whose superlative form, as Heidegger points out, is *deinotaton.* Most English translators I have consulted render the word as "wonder" or as "wondrous." Watling, for instance, in the Penguin classics edition, writes thus:

Wonders are many on earth, and the greatest of these
Is man.

However, any Greek-English dictionary lists many meanings for this word, including "strange" and "terrible," and it is safe to conclude that Heidegger's translation, slightly arbitrary like most of his renderings of the Greek, is not untrue to the spirit of the original. For the passage goes on to cite man's manifold accomplishments, such as his tireless attempts at mastery over Nature's creatures, his boldness in traversing earth and ocean, his discovery of language and the ability to rule over cities, to find cures for illness and to escape by daring and cunning the threats to his hegemony over beasts and natural forces. But with all his subtleties, the chorus reminds us, man has not learned how to avoid death, which conquers him and brings his work to nothing. And often he overreaches himself, falls into pride, and offends against the gods.

6. *Einführung in die Metaphysik* (Tübingen, 1953), p. 112.
7. *An Introduction to Metaphysics*, tr. by Ralph Manheim (New York, 1961), p. 123.

The passage is, in a sense, a celebration of man, justifying the adjective "wondrous." Yet the poet is not exalting human beings so much as expressing astonishment at this phenomenon and a feeling of awe, engendered both by man's accomplishments and his limitations. Man is not so much wonderful, in the modern sense of the term, as he is strange and inexplicable in power and in weakness. Hence Heidegger's rendering may well contain a basic justice, particularly if we keep the connotation of "homelessness" uppermost.

More to the point, however, is the way in which he now interprets the uncanniness or strangeness that Sophocles has discovered as basic to man's nature. The human creature is the strangest, the most homeless of beings because he responds with power and violence to the overwhelming power of Being itself. He refuses to yield to the panic fear that the vast spectacle of the world inspires in other creatures. Instead he ventures forth into the untried and unprecedented and explores "the extreme limits and abrupt abysses" [8] of his being-in-the-world. The secure abode of the familiar, the customary, the domestic he despises and rejects, preferring to do battle with the overpowering, strange, and terrible than to be at peace with the familiar.

Man experiences the uncanny, Heidegger is telling us here, both in himself and in the environing world because he refuses to accept his "place" and home in creation. "In willing the unprecedented he casts aside all help" [9] in order to gain a relationship to the powers that are beyond him. Man's homelessness makes him a creative being, puts him in touch with the Being to which he belongs, even if the cost be unbearably great.

It is not difficult to perceive in this work that the existentiality of the uncanny has taken on a more affirmative aspect than it possessed in *Being and Time*. There it pursued man

8. *Ibid.*, p. 125.
9. *Ibid.*, p. 137.

in his fallenness and inauthenticity as a threat. Here it lures him into the creative limits of his nature in order to allow him to realize his selfhood. Heidegger feels that in this poem Sophocles truly portrays man's violent, creative daring as a path to the essential truth of Being. Not-being-at-home in the already created is a necessary condition of actualizing human potentialities. Through self-assertion and travelling unexplored paths man can gain the closeness to Being that would be denied a creature who clung to the homelike and customary.

It is, however, in the "Letter on Humanism," 1947, and in certain essays of the untranslated volume, *Vorträge und Aufsätze*, 1954, that Heidegger's thoughts about the uncanny and about the nature of man generally reach their fuller and maturer development. These post-war writings do not represent so much a revision of his former work, in my judgment, as they do a completion of it and a certain change in emphasis. In his later life Heidegger pays increasing attention to the utterances of poets. And there is a notable lessening of polemical harshness; a kind of peace and tranquility seems to have settled upon his work with advancing age. One notes, too, in these post-war writings that the dogmatic tone is largely absent. "To ask questions is the piety of thought," he writes at the close of a recent essay.[10] It is apparent that he seeks to reflect, as simply as is possible for him, about basic questions, without the old assurance that he can provide any answers.

The "Letter on Humanism" will surely rank as one of the best things he has ever written. Though not always easy to understand, it is by no means as difficult as most of his writings. Often luminous in style, poetically conceived, it contains many of his philosophic concerns in their mature form. This essay is particularly relevant for my purpose, since its primary emphasis is on the nature of man.

Care, which is still the fundamental existentiality of man, is interpreted now in its more affirmative and hopeful aspects.

10. *Vorträge und Aufsätze* (Pfullingen, 1954), p. 44.

Yet the theme of uncanniness in the old sense of lostness in the inauthentic world is also very much present. Man is still for the most part and in his unreflective state forgetful of his true home in Being. "Homelessness," as Heidegger puts it, "becomes a world destiny." [11] The tendency of the individual to be completely absorbed by the public inauthentic world has even been heightened by the advance of technology and the mechanized life to which Western man has had to adjust. Everywhere individuals are directed toward single existents, fascinated by novelties, and urged to pass their days in forgetfulness of their deeper, contemplative nature.

Nevertheless, as this alienation of man from himself becomes more apparent, there is growing recognition of our plight. Heidegger feels that Marx, having discovered this principle of fundamental alienation of man, has given to his followers a view of history that is superior to most others in our time. Because they view man from the standpoint of the *history* of Being itself, that is Being in process, and not as do the phenomenologists and Jean-Paul Sartre from a static perspective, the Marxists are closer to the understanding of the modern age than the latter. This does not mean that Heidegger favors Marxism. He only finds it preferable to other alternatives. But Marxism is inadequate in its view of man because it is governed by a metaphysics which conceives man as a *homo faber* and assimilates him to the categorial kind of thinking appropriate only to the analysis of non-human beings. In Heidegger's judgment metaphysics, with its mistaken dichotomy between subject and object and its conception of man as a rational animal, continues to hold ascendancy over modern thought.

Though Heidegger is thus not more hopeful than formerly about the course of contemporary thought, he is nevertheless much clearer about the way existential man can escape this world destiny. Uncanniness no longer pursues man as a threat to his fallenness, as in *Being and Time*, nor does it serve as

11. "Letter on Humanism," p. 287.

an irresistible lure to drive him forcefully from the domestic
and secure, as in *Introduction to Metaphysics*. On the contrary, the state of not-being-at-home in the world can be
overcome by learning to dwell aright in closeness to Being.
To live is to dwell, as he now puts it, and many of his recent
attempts are directed toward describing the kind of home that
man can build on earth.

"Being," he writes in the "Letter on Humanism, "is the
transcendens as such." [12] Man is always in some fashion on
the way toward this transcending reality, seeking to dwell in
its vicinity. It is here clearly suggested that the genuinely existential man, alert to his potentialities, can come to be at home
in the world, rather than homeless and tormented by the uncanny. Man as a project cast off by Being into solitary and
singular consciousness has the possibility of return to the primal
source. The idea of *homecoming*, suggested so poignantly by
Hölderlin, Heidegger's favorite poet, takes on ontological significance in this and other recent essays.

Heidegger likes to speak of Being in these late essays in the
metaphor of a clearing (*Lichtung*) in the forest. The light
that such a clearing imparts enables man, scattered in the dark-
ness of the surrounding growth, and usually without forest
paths, to orient himself and to come nearer to the clearing.
The figure is reminiscent of Plato's imagery in the allegory of
the Cave. If man, says Heidegger in effect, is once again to
find himself in the neighborhood of this clearing, he must
learn to construct his own paths toward it.

Heidegger also uses the metaphor of a shepherd in attempting
to clarify man's relation to Being. "Man is not the master of
beings. Man is the shepherd of Being." [13] This metaphor is
employed by way of opposition to the "metaphysics of subjectivity" whereby everything is conceived in terms of its value

12. *Ibid.*, p. 285.
13. *Ibid.*, p. 288.

to human beings. There is, thinks Heidegger, something blas-
phemous in the modern attempt to interpret everything as a
value, an attempt which extends to the extreme of ranking
God as "man's highest value." In this measureless subjectivizing
of the real, there lies a kind of solipsism that is the reverse side
of the coin which interprets man as a utilitarian object, a
material thing to be used by whatever mindless power happens
to be dominant. The metaphor of the shepherd is Heidegger's
way of asserting, in ontological fashion, the dependence of man
on Being as such. The dignity of the shepherd rests on his
guarding and caring for that from which he derives his essential humanity. It is Heidegger's manner of insisting that we
can build a home for the spirit only when we have given up
the presumption that we are masters of the things that are.
Only when we understand ourselves as children of Care can
we gain that concern and solicitude for the earth and its multi-
farious inhabitants which will make us genuine householders.

IV

We may well ask at this point by what means Heidegger
conceives it possible to become once more at home in the
world. How can the genuine individual move away from the
uncanny and achieve the positive function of guardian which
serves to establish man's roots in Being?

His latest answers are again based on his profound appre-
ciation of the early Greeks. It is necessary, as he says, for
modern man to take a step backward in order to advance.
The Greek method of thinking, called *theoria*, has come more
and more to dominate his own thinking and to furnish him
with a method of philosophizing. *Theoria* he defines as "the
protective vision of truth." [14] It is as far removed as possible
from the logical and technological thinking which is designed
to make man master of Nature. On the contrary, *theoria*, now

14. *Vorträge und Aufsätze*, p. 53.

as in ancient times, is dominated by the desire for knowledge for its own sake. As a way of thinking it seeks to look upon the world as *physis* in the primordial sense, a vast phenomenon of process and change in which all parts are in some way interrelated and unified. The Greek vision which Heidegger seeks to revivify was essentially an aesthetic method of thinking, if one understands by "aesthetic" its original sense as a seeing, concrete and objective. It was objective in not seeking to interpret Nature in terms of what the viewer contributed; concrete, in not separating the seen as mere appearance from a presumed "reality" which lay behind it. Such seeing was, on the contrary, content to "let things be" and to perceive them in their integrity and independence.

This aesthetic way of thinking and inquiry, Heidegger believes, knows how to ask questions truly, as it knows how to listen for the answers and to wait, however long the answers may be in coming. It is a disposition of reverent attention to the essence of the simplest and most ordinary things and experiences. *Theoria* is also a kind of commemorative thinking, a thinking that is at one and the same time a thanking. For the world can be to us as it was to those early Greeks a marvelous phenomenon. To understand it truly is to be filled with wonder. Hence philosophy is closely allied with poetry. Both can provide man with a house and a home. "Poetry is the original dwelling," as Heidegger puts it in a recent essay on Hölderlin; "poetry is man's basic ability to dwell humanly on earth." [15] Elsewhere he adds that "dwelling is the principal characteristic of Being in relation to mortals." [16]

Central, therefore, to the understanding of Heidegger's recent image of man is his emphasis on this meditative, poetic vision as the mode by which men approach the truth about themselves as members of the realm of Being. Being is through and through historical, that is, active, in process of becoming,

15. *Ibid.*, pp. 202, 203.
16. *Ibid.*, p. 161.

inexhaustible in its variety, and in the features it presents for our contemplation. As its creature man is accordingly never completed or completable. His image as a species is not fixed and hence can never be known once and for all. He is always *underway*, a favorite term of Heidegger's, in process of realizing his unique potentialities. The best way to achieve these is to adopt the questioning attitude, the stance of a meditative listener as well as an inquirer who understands truth as an uncovering of the reality of things in a way that will reveal the essence or presence (*Wesen, Anwesenheit*) of Being and the human essence or presence at one and the same time.

The procedure that covers up this truth, Heidegger thinks, is the contemporary predilection for exploitation, best exemplified in technology and a scientific mentality that regards everything in the world as there for us. Such a mentality is a natural consequence of a metaphysics that starts from the analysis of man as a rational animal, separated from the world about him by his possession of consciousness that stands in absolute contrast to objects in that world. This mentality generates an egocentrism that makes impossible any union of the human being with the more inclusive Being of the world. Ontological thinking, in contrast, lets things be in their own nature, not out of indifference or lack of concern for their function, but because only so can man build his dwelling and live well in the neighborhood of the "clearing."

Letting things be will also enable man to bring their essence and truth into language. Heidegger's conception of language is at the opposite pole from that of his contemporary, Ludwig Wittgenstein, who taught that man's greatest effort must be expended "to prevent the bewitchment of our intelligence by means of our language." "What, *we* do," wrote Wittgenstein, "is to bring words back from their metaphysical to their everyday usage." [17] Some of the analytic philosophers are con-

17. *Philosophical Investigations*, tr. by G. E. M. Anscombe (Oxford and New York, 1953), p. 48e.

cerned to clear out the meaningless words from our use of language. Such a conception is foreign to Heidegger. Though he too is hostile to metaphysics, he looks upon language, or more correctly, the spoken and the written *word,* as a near-miraculous creation. To conceive it, as do the analysts, as a conceptual tool of human intelligence, is radically to mistake effect for cause.

Language makes man what he is, namely, human, and not the other way around. Though men imagine that they are masters of language, in reality language forms and masters us, says Heidegger. As he puts it in the "Humanism" letter, "Language is the house of Being." [18] Just as Being controls man, not the reverse, so does language, by means of which we grasp that Being, make us what we are. Through speech man is separated by an abyss from all other creatures. Animals are essentially "worldless," whereas we dwell by way of communication and participation in the truth of Being. If poets and thinkers are able to strip away the encrustations that thoughtless use has fastened on words and get back to their primordial meaning, they will discover, so Heidegger believes, that language is truly a kind of house in which Being dwells.

Toward the close of the "Letter on Humanism" Heidegger comments on a charming and profound story about Heraclitus, found in Aristotle, which perhaps best sums up this new approach of his to the existentialities of human nature.

> An anecdote tells of an explanation that Heraclitus is said to have given strangers who wanted to approach him. Upon approaching they found him warming himself at a stove. They stopped surprised and all the more so because as they hesitated he encouraged them and bade them come in with the words: "For here too there are gods present." [19]

The visitors are imagined by Heidegger as inquisitive and

18. "Letter on Humanism," p. 271.
19. *Ibid.,* p. 296.

expecting the sensational. They hope to discover the thinker in a stance of profound meditation among appropriate surroundings. Instead they find him in a hut, warming himself beside a cookstove. Their disappointment is great. "The glimpse of a freezing thinker offers little of interest. And so the inquisitive ones . . . lose their desire to come any closer. What are they to do there? This ordinary dull event of someone cold and standing by the stove one can find any time in his own home." [20] But Heraclitus heartens them and urges them to enter with the observation that even here the gods are present.

Heidegger tells this story as a partial answer to Jean Beaufret's question about the relation of ontology to a possible ethics. It was Heraclitus who asserted in an extant fragment, "*ēthos anthrōpō daimōn*," usually translated as "a man's character is his daimon." Heidegger insists that *ēthos* means abode or dwelling and that *daimōn* here signifies God. Hence Heraclitus is saying that "Man, insofar as he is man, dwells in the nearness of God." [21]

By this cryptic reply to Beaufret's question, Heidegger wants to suggest that the question of practice or ethics in today's world cannot be separated from the question of theory or *theoria*. He assures his interrogator that problems of conduct are crucially important in this age of mass society and technology, where confusion and perplexity pass all bounds. But the temptation to set up rules of conduct without an understanding of man's relation to Being must be resisted. The kind of thinking that is ontological, and which the fragment of Heraclitus as well as the anecdote about him illustrate, is prior to the distinction between theory and practice. When man learns to dwell as a neighbor of Being, Heidegger is saying in effect, he will also know how to conduct his moral life. His thinking will be a form of action and his action a form of

20. *Ibid.*, p. 297.
21. *Ibid.*, p. 296.

thinking. Like Heraclitus, he will know that in whatever circumstances he finds himself, the gods are present even there.

At this point the question is inevitable: To what extent is
Heidegger's image of man a religious one? Is his notion of
Being at all compatible with the Christian conception of God?

There is considerable disagreement about the answers to
these questions. On the one hand, many Catholic theologians
have long been interested in Heidegger, who was brought up
a Catholic and devoted an early book (1916) to Duns Scotus.
Furthermore, the tone of many of his post-war writings is
deeply contemplative, sometimes approaching the mystical. On
the other hand, American commentators frequently class him
with Sartre as an atheistic existentialist.

Some of the confusion on this matter is needless, in my
opinion, for Heidegger has himself spoken out on it explicitly
in the "Letter on Humanism" and indeed long before that. He
points out in the "Letter" that the charge of atheism is ground-
less, since as early as 1929 in a footnote on the short essay,
"Das Wesen des Grundes," he had declared: "Through the
ontological interpretation of *Dasein* [the human way of being]
as Being-in-the-world, there is neither a positive nor a negative
resolution of a possible Being-towards-God. However, through
the elucidation of the transcendency there is first obtained *an
adequate concept of Dasein*, in consideration of which one
may now ask what exactly is, ontologically, the relationship
between God and *Dasein*." [22]

Heidegger complains that this significant remark (the italics
are his own) has been wrongly taken as indicating indifference
on his part toward religion, an indifference that would inevitably lead to nihilism. Such, he asserts, was and is furthest from
his intention. On the contrary, he regards his attempt to think
the nature of man ontologically as a groundwork on which

22. *Ibid.,* p. 294.

theology could construct an adequate conception of the divine
and the holy. Nevertheless, he cautions, this does not mean
that his philosophy wishes to declare itself for theism any
more than for atheism. It fails to do so not out of indifference
to the question but because philosophical thought must observe
its limits and cannot take a stand on the Being of God.

Is his conception of man, then, a humanistic one? Beaufret
had asked him how one could restore a meaning to the term
"humanism" and a large part of the "Letter" is devoted to a
reply to this question. Heidegger rejects at least the usual interpretations of humanism as a designation for his understanding
of human nature. The reason is that humanism, originally a
Roman designation, derives from the false metaphysics that conceives man in the usual way as a rational animal. Such humanism, Heidegger observes, may be rightly concerned with establishing man's dignity and asserting humane social and political
values. In opposing it he does not thereby accept the charges
that his conception is irrational, inhumane, illogical, and opposed to values. There is a position that is neither humanistic
in this sense nor anti-human. The difficulty with the Roman
conception of *humanitas* is that it does not rate the dignity of
man highly enough, since it conceives him as distinguished
from other animals only by the addition of reason. More importantly, the usual humanism mistakes the essence of human
nature by presumptuously interpreting man as lord of all Being,
to which everything must be subject. Against this metaphysics
of subjectivity Heidegger insists in putting forth his "fundamental ontology."

However, if humanism be conceived in an extreme sense
whereby man's *humanitas* consists in his allegiance to Being
itself and his attempts to come close to It in a protective and
cherishing way and to give It voice in language, then Heidegger
would call himself a true humanist. He puts this standpoint
well, both poetically and philosophically, in the final paragraph

of the "Letter." It is worth quoting, in the translation of Edgar
Lohner.

> Future thought is no longer philosophy, because it thinks
> more originally than metaphysics. But neither can future
> thought, as Hegel demanded, lay aside the name "love of
> wisdom" and become wisdom itself in the form of absolute
> knowledge. Thought is on its descent to the poverty of its
> provisional essence. Thought gathers language in simple
> speech. Language is thus the language of Being, as the clouds
> are the clouds of the sky. Thought by its speaking traces
> insignificant furrows in language. They seem even more
> insignificant than the furrows the peasant with deliberate steps
> traces in the field.[23]

The answer to the question of whether Heidegger's image
of man is a possible Christian one has, I think, been answered
in the negative. His standpoint is religious in the sense that
man is bound to a higher Being than himself, toward which
he is when authentically himself constantly transcending. But
this Being of Heidegger's is pre-Christian or non-Christian in
substance. For it is an ancient Hellenic vision of the Divine.
Heidegger's whole philosophy, as I interpret it, stands under
the influence of the pre-classical Greek interpretation of reality, however mistaken his grasp of the fragment of that civil-
ization we possess may be. Unlike Hegel, who attempted to
synthesize Greek and Christian interpretations, Heidegger has
rejected, I think, the essential elements of Christian theology
as well as the main outlines of the Christian understanding of
man. And this in spite of the fact that many of his analyses
of human existentialities have a decidedly Christian flavor,
giving rise to the temptation to interpret them as a secularized
version of Christianity. This is a temptation that, as Heidegger
himself has indicated, should be resisted.

23. *Ibid.*, p. 302.

V

In conclusion, I may be permitted to make a general comment about the Heideggerian image of man. Heidegger is a philosopher toward whom it is difficult to remain neutral in attitude. I have been trying to understand his thinking now for some fifteen years and have had opportunities to speak with him at length. Despite this I am, like most commentators, far from sure that I grasp what he is about. His writings are full of pitfalls for the interpreter, and it is hazardous to assent to or dissent from a position you are not sure you understand.

An old school friend of his and a fellow philosopher remarked to me some years ago, in effect, since I do not remember his exact phrasing: "Heidegger says a lot of foolish things. His writings are often full of nonsense. But I am not interested in these. What does concern me are the things that he writes that are really good and true." On reflection this observation seems to me sound and very wise. One remembers that most of the philosophers in the Western tradition have written a lot of nonsense which is woven inextricably into their best thoughts. Naturally this does not make Heidegger a great philosopher, but it should caution us to look for what is usable in him for our own philosophizing and let the foolishness go.

Despite his frequent obscurity, Heidegger's image of man seems to me fairly clear in main outline, as well as important and original. There is profundity in his characterization of man as that being who is concerned about his own being. Since this concern is never finally stilled in the short span each of us lives and since man appears only as an individualized consciousness, no final definition of human nature is possible. I have come to agree with Heidegger that because our human way of being is so inextricably bound up with the being of others as well as with the being of things and creatures of Nature, the attempt to understand man as a distinct being is misguided. Finally, I believe that Heidegger is profoundly correct in seeking to pursue the partial understanding of man that is possible for us by a revival of the old Greek *theoria* as a method of inquiry in more or less conscious contrast with scientific methods of analysis. By so doing we may partly overcome the widespread and unhappy alienation of our day and learn to live better in the sense of gaining closer attachments to the natural environment and even to our fellow men.

Sein und Zeit, Halle, 1927.
—Translation by John Macquarrie and Edward Robinson, *Being and Time*, London and New York, 1962.
Kant und das Problem der Metaphysik, Bonn, 1929.
—Translation by James S. Churchill, *Kant and the Problem of Metaphysics*, Bloomington, 1962.
"Vom Wesen des Grundes," in *Festschrift für E. Husserl*, Halle, 1929; also published separately, Frankfurt am Main, 1949.
Was ist Metaphysik?, Bonn, 1929.
—Translation by R. F. C. Hull and Alan Crick, "What is Metaphysics?" in *Existence and Being*, ed. Werner Brock, Chicago, 1949.
—Translation of the "Einleitung" (1949) by Walter Kaufmann, "The Way Back into the Ground of Metaphysics," in *Existentialism from Dostoevsky to Sartre*, New York, 1956, pp. 207-221.
Hölderlin und das Wesen der Dichtung, Munich, 1937.
—Translation by Douglas Scott, "Hölderlin and the Essence of Poetry," in *Existence and Being*, *op. cit.*
Vom Wesen der Wahrheit, Frankfurt, 1943.
—Translation by R. F. C. Hull and Alan Crick, "On the Essence of Truth," in *Existence and Being*, *op. cit.*
Platons Lehre von der Wahrheit with "Brief über den Humanismus," Bern, 1947.
—Translation by John Barlow, "Plato's Doctrine of Truth" and by Edgar Lohner, "Letter on Humanism," in *Philosophy in the Twentieth Century*, ed. William Barrett and Henry D. Aiken, New York, Vol. II, 1962.
Holzwege, Frankfurt, 1950.
—Translation of the second essay by Marjorie Grene, "The Age of the World View," in *Measure* (1951), pp. 269-284.
Erläuterungen zu Hölderlins Dichtung, 2nd ed., Frankfurt, 1951.
Einführung in die Metaphysik, Tübingen, 1953.
—Translation by Ralph Manheim, *An Introduction to Metaphysics*, New Haven, 1959; New York, 1961.
Was Heisst Denken? Tübingen, 1954.
Vorträge und Aufsätze, Pfullingen, 1954.

Zur Seinsfrage, Frankfurt, 1955.

—Translation by William Kluback and Jean T. Wilde, *The Question of Being*, London and New York, 1958.

Was ist das—die Philosophie? Pfullingen, 1956.

—Translation by William Kluback and Jean T. Wilde, *What is Philosophy?* London and New York, 1958.

Der Satz vom Grund, Pfullingen, 1957.

Identität und Differenz, Pfullingen, 1957.

—Translation by Kurt F. Leidecker, *Essays in Metaphysics: Identity and Difference*, New York, 1960.

Unterwegs zur Sprache, Pfullingen, 1959.

Nietzsche, 2 vols., Pfullingen, 1961.

Die Technik und die Kehre, Pfullingen, 1962.

Die Frage nach dem Ding: Zu Kants Lehre von den transzendentalen Grundsätzen, Tübingen, 1962.

HENRY S. HARRIS

The "Modernity" of Franco Lombardi

AN ESSAY IN CONTEMPORARY ITALIAN PHILOSOPHY

I

What Marx said of capitalist society may perhaps be said of philosophy—at least in the "capitalist" world—with more evident truth: to wit, that it produces its own gravediggers. For this reason it is certainly foolish to speak of an "age of transition" in philosophy, since every period of philosophical activity worthy of the name is a transitional period. But there are times when it seems as if a philosophical funeral has ended, no new hearse or coffin is to be seen and yet the assembled company, whether sextons or mourners, do not leave the churchyard but linger disconsolately as if uncertain what to

*Since its first reading, before the American Philosophical Association, this paper has been revised slightly in the light of comments and criticisms offered by Professor Lombardi himself, some of which are referred to specifically in the footnotes.

do next. No genuine *transition* has occurred and it seems that a new *beginning* must be made; but it remains uncertain when that beginning will take place or what it will prove to be the beginning of.

This seems to me to be very nearly the case in Italian philosophy at the present time. The funeral of idealism began to be proclaimed almost as soon as Gentile began his university career with an inaugural lecture announcing its rebirth and Croce founded *La Critica* (both events occurring in 1903). But as events turned out it was not really philosophy professors who dug the grave, although it became the customary thing for every fledgling professor to mark his maturity by proclaiming that he had in one way or another "overcome" the idealists. Italian idealism died in Mussolini's wars—in the electoral violence of the *squadristi* in 1924, in Abyssinia, in the assault on France, and in the civil war of 1943.

Gentile's apology for the *squadristi* was the beginning of the end. Croce condemned what he called the "philosophical cretinism" of Gentile's stand; and it seemed for a time that Gentile, for his part, would be able to justify his opposition to the dictatorship established in 1925 without abandoning his idealist faith in history. As he viewed it then, Fascism was no more than a parenthesis, a regrettable interlude in the history of the Italian spirit. But the Abyssinian crisis found him already wavering, inclined to think of Fascism as more truly the agent of the Spirit than were the abstract theorists of international justice at Geneva; and the intervention in 1940 left him faced with the choice, at once unbearable and unavoidable, between Fascist victory and Italian defeat—a choice that clearly revealed the inadequacy of his "parenthetical" conception of Fascism.[1]

Hence the end of the war in Europe and the dawn of a

1. For the relations and attitudes of Gentile and Croce during the Fascist period, see my *Social Philosophy of Giovanni Gentile* (Urbana, 1960), Chapters VI and VII.

new era at Hiroshima found Italy almost without intellectual resources. France and Germany, who, though they had suffered at least as much, had philosophers ready at hand with concepts adequate at least for the *diagnosis* of the disaster, jointly assumed the intellectual hegemony of the new Europe; and in England the pre-war axis of Vienna and Cambridge passed over into a somewhat volatile synthesis with the almost defunct tradition of idealism and the perennial tradition of classical humanism at Oxford to produce what many among us like to think of as a genuine renaissance in philosophy, a movement which certainly possesses the hegemony of the English-speaking world, though it, too, is not without gravediggers and obituary writers on all sides.

Italy's unreadiness to contribute to the new situation can be traced in part to political causes.[2] The academic and cultural world of Italy has always tended to be a faithful image of its political life, ever since, more than a hundred years ago, Francesco DeSanctis, the most prominent philosophical and

2. Professor Lombardi has remarked to me that my interpretation of Italian philosophical development is "too directly political." He points out that, "at least down to 1938, the situation in Italy was much less influenced by politics than was the case, for example, under Nazism; one has only to reflect that my book on Feuerbach was allowed to come out in 1935." His point is well taken. A political interpretation of the currents in Italian philosophy can only produce a very crude simplification of the truth. But I hope the reader will realize that no comparison of the situation in Italy with that in Nazi Germany was ever intended. My point is that philosophy in Italy does have a political dimension which it generally lacks in the English-speaking world. Of course, we have philosophers who are politically oriented (just as Italy has some who are not); we have even had movements or schools (like utilitarianism in England or the instrumentalism of Dewey in America) with a characteristic political tendency. But at the moment, certainly, one could not even produce a recognizable caricature of our philosophical situation in political terms. It may therefore be of some value to English-speaking readers to have this aspect of Italian philosophy pointed out, since they might otherwise overlook it; and since an extremely simplified perspective is all that I can hope to provide here in any case, I have chosen the political perspective as being more germane to the present topic than any other.

literary figure of the newborn nation, began as its first minister of education to purge supporters of the *ancien régime* from academic life. DeSanctis' political action formed a precedent to which Gentile pointed in 1925, when the Fascists began a purge of the same kind which culminated in the notorious oath of allegiance to the Regime imposed on university professors in 1931. Although Gentile had resigned from his cabinet post as early as 1924, he always remained the figurehead of "Fascist culture," and actually provided the official political theory of the Regime. Given the system of appointment to professorial chairs, it is not surprising to find that his school established a virtual stranglehold on the higher academic posts.

It must be emphasized that there was nothing very new about this kind of monopoly, except that it extended over a greater range than before. Moreover, it was necessarily a temporary phenomenon whose duration depended upon the school's vitality, which could not be maintained without the heresies and splits that philosophical vitality always involves. What was *really* disastrous was that the political dictatorship tended to reduce all argument about current affairs to the level of purely verbal and *academic* discussion. In the "Fascist culture" that was proclaimed as the Regime entered its second decade there were only two issues that still showed a spark of life: the reconciliation of the Regime with the Church, and the creation of the Corporate State. There was, of course, no unavoidable incoherence or conflict between these two Fascist achievements; but, in point of fact, the parties that gathered to defend, interpret, and develop them were in large measure convinced that the true spirit of Fascism was to be found in only one of them, and that the other was no more than a necessary evil at best. Thus the idealists crystallized into two groups: the "right," whose leaders belonged to the first generation to fall under Gentile's influence, and who now labored for a *rapprochement* between idealism and Catholicism, and the "left," led by the second generation, who devoted themselves to the problems of Fascist syndicalism and corporate economics.

At about the same time (c. 1930) the opposed currents of German philosophy represented by Heidegger and the Vienna Circle began to penetrate across the Alps. This was largely through the efforts of thinkers who had always been opposed to the idealists, and thus implies a qualification of what was said earlier about the idealist stranglehold on academic life; but in this connection it deserves to be noted that the secular wing of the existentialist movement in Italy was from the beginning in fairly sympathetic alliance with the supporters of positivism and scientific methodology. This phenomenon, unparalleled, as far as I know, in the rest of the world, is itself evidence of the overwhelming influence of idealism, since the only thing that the two trends had in common, at least initially, was the feeling that in advancing their claims, whether of human individuality or of empiricism and scientific method, they were both alike reasserting the concreteness of values which the historicism of Croce and Gentile had reduced to the status of abstractions.

The fall of Fascism and the assassination of Gentile abolished this basic pattern of affairs almost overnight, and created a tremendous hiatus for nearly all Italian philosophers outside the ambit of the Church. New problems had to be found, new goals set up, and new alignments established. Italy was no longer a self-sufficient, if not quite windowless, monad. Under the aegis of the alliance between scientific methodologists and existentialists the first postwar generation of students began to study and publicize contemporary developments in Anglo-American philosophy, while on the old idealist "left" there was a marked upsurge of interest in Marxism.[3] The widespread

3. The currents of French Catholic existentialism mingled easily with the work of the idealist "right" to produce "Christian spiritualism." For this group, as for the perennial Thomistic tradition, the hiatus of 1943-44 was much less serious.

interest aroused by the publication of Franco Lombardi's book, *Birth of the Modern World*, in 1953 is, in part at least, a symptom of this last-mentioned development.[4]

II

Lombardi is emphatically not a doctrinaire Marxist, but he comes from a family of socialist intellectuals, and by his own account cut his philosophical teeth at the *liceo* by trying to provide an account of dialectical materialism that was consistent with human freedom and responsibility in political action. It would almost be fair to say that this has remained the fundamental aim in all of his subsequent philosophizing, though he was not himself conscious of it for a long time. At the university, and for some years thereafter, his philosophical interest was focussed upon Croce's *Aesthetic* and Gentile's *Logic;* his own thought first came to maturity as a critique of the idealist doctrine of a Universal Spirit, and an attempt to disentangle the proper, strictly human, meaning of the idealist account of experience. In 1934, while he was still working on the first systematic statement of his views, he was awarded a fellowship for study in Germany; subsequently he remained there for a number of years as lecturer (first at Marburg and later at Frankfurt). In Germany he wrote a book on Feuerbach (1935) and then the first book in Italian on Kierkegaard (1936). These two figures seem to symbolize for him the fundamental "either-or" of philosophy after Hegel, and even before he began to write on either of them he had opted decisively for Feuerbach. This was shown by the fact that he borrowed the title of his "system" from Feuerbach. It appeared in 1935 in two parts: *Experience and Man* (theory of knowledge) and *The World of Men* (theory of action); but he has indicated that this second title was properly the title of the whole work.[5]

4. *Nascita del mondo moderno* (Asti, 1953; now Rome). Hereafter, *Nascita.*
5. See the first four entries in the Lombardi bibliography below, p. 86.

In 1943 he threw himself enthusiastically into clandestine propaganda work for the Italian Socialist Party, reborn among the partisans; and he continued to take an active part in political life until the party split into the two factions still headed by Nenni and Saragat, a rupture which to him meant the end of the only truly progressive force in Italian politics.[6] The "birth of the modern world" (or of "the world of men"), which he looks for, is something which can only take place when and if the polarization of political life into a "right" which is not conservative or reactionary and a "left" which is not liberal or progressive can be overcome. Our concepts have become confused and ambiguous; we can no longer agree on how to apply them to the present situation.

When it is viewed against this background, *Nascita del mondo moderno* is the proper contribution of a philosopher to the "birth of the modern world"; an attempt to clarify the fundamental political concepts of "modernity" or "progress" as opposed to "reaction." But Professor Lombardi does not examine these concepts in a narrowly political context. His political concern is apparent in the introduction and again in the concluding part of the book; but the core of his discussion is a consideration, in the broadest terms, of what should be thought of as distinctively *modern* in "modern philosophy." From this point of view the best way to characterize the book briefly is to say that it seeks to overthrow the conception of the history of philosophy which almost all of us, in one form or another, have inherited from Hegel, who was the real founder of the history of philosophy as a discipline. It is natural enough that Lombardi should view his task in this way since he wants eventually to provide a *philosophy* for the "modern world," and he was Professor of the *History* of Philosophy at Rome until 1956 (in which year he advanced to the chair of Moral Philosophy); but it must be said that the connections between the socio-political analysis of our present crisis and the philosophical-historical analysis of the concept

6. Cf. *Nascita*, pp. 42-43.

of "modernity" are not clearly delineated, and perhaps *cannot* be delineated without some modifications on the philosophical side. The book is rather like a badly designed insect whose head and abdomen were not conceived at the same time as the thoracic machinery and wings that keep it alive and in flight.[7] Nonetheless, as Philip Leon said in reviewing it for *Mind* (1955), it is clearly "a work of prime importance." It has already been translated into French and German.[8]

As Professor Findlay has recently reminded us,[9] the spirit of the "modern" world was for Hegel identical with the "spirit" of Christianity; and this view does in a way correspond to, and offer a more or less plausible account of, one ordinary use of the expression "modern world"—the one in which it is opposed to "ancient world." Lombardi begins by criticizing this view in some detail, but we can sum up this part of his argument more or less adequately by saying that he takes the opposition between "modern" and "medieval" to be more fundamental than that between "modern" and "ancient." The notion of "modernity" properly came to birth in the Renaissance, and the "modern" spirit is essentially closer to the "naturalism" of the ancients than to the Christian ideal which dominated the medieval period.

Those who know their Hegel may here be tempted to argue that he would have no quarrel with this historical thesis, since for him the "modern world" meant the "Christian German world," i.e., not the whole Christian era but the post-Reformation period. The spirit of Christianity was for Hegel the spirit of Protestantism, not that of the Catholic Church; he had no sympathy with the medieval yearnings of some of his romantic contemporaries. He would have been the first to grant that the early Christian protest against the pagan schools of philosophy was not a philosophical reaction at all, and that when the new

7. The author's note on the writing of the book (p. 315) does in fact reveal that different parts were written at different times and for differing occasions.

8. See bibliography below, p. 86.

9. Cf. *Hegel: A Re-Examination* (London, 1958), pp. 30, 354, etc.

faith did rise to a philosophical level it only did so by borrowing the forms of classical intellectualism.

Lombardi's critique of Hegel seems therefore to be unjust in that he never seriously considers Hegel's view that the "Middle" ages were in fact just that, i.e., a period of transition between "ancient" and "modern." This oversight of his is a pity because it obscures the real point at issue between them, which concerns the relative importance for modern culture of the Renaissance as against the Reformation.[10] In Lombardi's view the Reformation and Counter-Reformation are precisely a reaction *against* the "modern" humanist spirit of the Renaissance; Hegel is right, he seems to think, in finding the fullest development of the Christian spirit here, because here the protest against the ancient schools is finally raised to full self-consciousness. The Catholic compromise between faith and reason is now decisively rejected, and the Christian spirit reveals itself for what it is: the absolute antithesis of "modernity," of progress, and of faith in "the world of men." Lombardi contrasts the Christian protest on behalf of faith against knowledge, and on behalf of personal salvation against the disinterested search for truth, with Bacon's protest on behalf of scientific practical reason and human control of nature against the classical contemplative spirit. The disinterested search for truth he takes as typifying the whole western historical progressive tradition as opposed to the quest for personal salvation which originates in the more static cultures of the East.[11]

In the religious quest for salvation, the knowledge of this

10. It should be emphasized that this is my way of stating the issue, not Lombardi's. He has pointed out to me that what he seeks to bring out in his book is that Hegel did not even *have the concept* of the "Renaissance," because it was in the main constructed by later historians. (cf. *Nascita*, p. 78) Without wanting to quibble about "possession of the concept," I think there is clear evidence in Hegel's writings that he distinguished between a secular and a religious breach with medieval Christendom; just as he explicitly distinguished between the secular (French) and the religious (German) Enlightenment that followed. This is enough to validate the contrast I am seeking to draw here.

11. *Nascita*, pp. 65-66.

world becomes a delusion and the joys of this life a snare. The "world" and the "flesh" form the first two terms of an infernal trinity, so to speak, whose third member or "spirit" is none other than the devil himself. The contribution of the Renaissance to the modern world lies precisely in the restoration of a positive attitude to nature, a reaffirmation of the world and the flesh. The modern morality is one of human dignity and self-realization, whereas even Kant, who must presumably be regarded as the greatest of Protestant Christian moralists, is accused by Lombardi of offering only a "morality for slaves." [12]

The humanistic naturalism which makes the Renaissance "modern," in contrast with both the medieval Catholicism that preceded and the Protestant reform that followed, is only the first of four phases or strands which Lombardi distinguishes in the concept of modernity. The second is provided by the scientific revolution and the Enlightenment. Here again the foundation was laid through the revival of a classical tradition: the atheistic materialism of the Atomists. But more important than the new conception of the physical world was the spread of what Lombardi calls the "scientific mentality": the attitude of critical rationalism that is common to the rationalists strictly so-called and to the empiricists. The triumph of this mentality over the whole range of human experience (even, for example, in religion) is what typifies the "Enlightenment." The faith in progress which is the fundamental value of modernity has its origin here.[13]

In virtue of its faith in the universal empire, the omnicompetence of human reason, the Enlightenment was more "mod-

12. *Ibid.*, p. 68.

13. It is noteworthy, however, that what we are accustomed to think of as the high peaks of "rationalism" in philosophy (e.g., the *Ethics* of Spinoza) are regarded by Lombardi as the weak non-modern side of the Enlightenment, since they rest on the theory of innate ideas and culminate in the reactionary Platonic-theological ideal of contemplating the *eternal* truth.

ern" than the Romantic era to which it gave place. But the conservative reaction of the Romantics in favor of custom and tradition, and the unconscious wisdom enshrined in institutions, was the unavoidable cost of an understanding of human freedom in history, which is the necessary correction of abstract rationalism and forms the third phase of modernity. The Enlightenment on its side laid the foundation for this new understanding by establishing the principle of toleration. The connection between toleration of heresy and the freedom of doubt and inquiry necessary for rational progress and enlightenment is easy to see;[14] on the other side, the fact that it was only accepted in the aftermath of bitter wars and persecutions involving all the various Christian sects is apparently proof enough for Lombardi that the spirit of Christianity is the spirit of *in*tolerance.[15]

The Romantic period exalted the inward subjective emotions as against the impersonal world of scientific reason. It glorified intuition, spontaneity, and made immediacy the criterion of absolute value. But this cult of immediacy led to a quest for origins and so to a new dimension of rational inquiry: historical reason. Thus, insofar as it combined with the rational spirit of the Enlightenment to produce the liberal nationalism of the nineteenth century Romanticism was itself progressive and "modern." But insofar as it looked back to the medieval period for its ideals it became a new form of theological reaction, all the more dangerous because it was masquerading as the spirit of historical development and progress. Human freedom was swallowed up once again in the inexorable "march of God in the world." The truest representative of the new historical consciousness on its modern progressive side was therefore not Hegel, or even Marx, but Darwin.[16] The philosophy of this

14. Spinoza here again provides a perfect example—both in his life and in his writings.

15. Cf. *Nascita*, p. 94.

16. *Ibid.*, p. 100.

period, inasmuch as it becomes alienated from science, is reactionary.

These first three phases in the development of the "modern world," Renaissance, Enlightenment, Romanticism, are relatively easy to characterize. But Lombardi holds that there is a fourth stage, a "silent revolution," which has been going on in our own century. This is hard to expound because we are so close to it, and because the concepts to express it have yet to be formulated. *Birth of the Modern World* is itself an essay in this direction and the "silent revolution" will not be successfully consummated until a really "modern" philosophy exists. But it is not just a matter of the modern spirit finally rising to self-consciousness. A social revolution has occurred. We have lost the traditional faith in progress which both the Enlightenment and the Romantic period in their different ways possessed, but we have a new faith in humanity and in private happiness; partly in spite of, and partly by means of, the totalitarian forms of modern life we are seeking to defend the absolute value of the individual person. Totalitarianism is itself the reactionary aspect of this new world, and the ambiguity and corruption of the traditional concepts and values of liberal humanism are brought about by the tacit consciousness that there cannot be *any* privileged individuals, groups, or nations in the new era now beginning. The autonomous rational individual of the Enlightenment gave way to the autonomy of the nation state, and this in turn is now giving way to a mass democracy that transcends national boundaries. The ideals of modernity all point towards a universal social democracy, and therefore we cannot simply take our stand *against* the totalitarian tendencies of modern society without becoming ourselves reactionary defenders of social privilege. The traditional values must somehow be defended and preserved in and through the new social forms. Lombardi believes the necessary mediating principle is to be found in "a new sense of the social nature of man and of the solidarity of humanity in every single individual." [17]

Precisely because since 1939 we have entered a new era the need for a genuinely modern philosophy has become more pressing than ever before. The stage of history is no longer Europe but the world; and the unit of historical action, not the nation but the continent. But progress is not an inevitable necessity, and there can be little hope of preserving what has been achieved by the modern national communities unless their heritage is correctly understood. Lombardi seems to hold that no philosophy has hitherto been fully modern. Even at its best, in the Enlightenment, philosophy was as much reactionary as it was progressive, and the present confusion of our ideas and values arises in part from the fact that the Romantic philosophy was far more reactionary than progressive.

The concern of philosophy, according to Lombardi, has always been with something which he calls the "pure concept"; for any region of thought or action, the "pure concept," if I understand him rightly, is the concept through which we can comprehend *all* of the actual and possible phenomena in that range of experience. Thus in the theory of knowledge the fundamental problem is to define "thinking" in such a way as to account satisfactorily not merely for true thought but also for erroneous thought; or to put the problem another way, we must define "reason" in such a way that error remains intellectually respectable, and does not have to be dismissed as the work of some alien force (the "will" being the obvious candidate).[18]

This is just what philosophers in general have failed to do. From Plato onwards they conceived of knowledge as the intel-

17. *Ibid.,* p. 102.

18. *Ibid.,* pp. 183-214. Lombardi's most recent statement of "philosophy as the pure concept" is in *Il piano del nostro sapere* (Rome, 1958), pp. 41-75.

lectual intuition of an independent reality, so that either *all* thought is true thought and error must arise from some other source (the extreme of absolute rationalism that begins with Plato) or truth is unattainable and all thought is erroneous (the extreme of skeptical empiricism that begins in the next generation of the Academy). The root of the trouble lies in the belief that the object of knowledge must be known simply *as it is* in itself, so that cognition becomes an immediate all-or-nothing affair. Truth thus becomes a theological concept, since to know something means to share in God's view of it. For this reason philosophers have inevitably suffered from the essential theological vice of intolerance; and it is in this respect that the reactionary character of previous philosophy is most immediately apparent. But in reality the theological conception of absolute truth is *absolutely* (and not just in this respect) antithetical to the modern ideal of the free individual human personality. Philosophy will not begin to be modern until it accepts the starting point offered by Kierkegaard's complaint against Hegel: "There is no absolute thought, there is only an individual who thinks." [19]

Kant's philosophy represents the conscious recognition of the dilemma of theological truth. For he contrives to be at once an absolute rationalist with respect to human thought (the categories of possible experience) and an absolute skeptic with respect to independent reality (the thing in itself). Once his successors had rejected the skeptical, defeatist side of his thought, philosophy became explicitly what (on the positive side) it had always been implicitly—an attempt to join in the self-contemplation of Aristotle's God. Yet in the Kantian revolution, thus perverted into the worst form of theological speculation, lay the seeds of a truly human conception of thought,

19. Lombardi cites the phrase frequently: e.g., in *Nascita*, p. 201, and in *Ricostruzione filosofica* (Asti, 1956; now Rome), p. 26. For the fullest exposition of his critique of the ideal of objective truth see *Le origini della filosofia europea nel mondo greco* (Asti, 1954; now Rome).

and under all the theological camouflage of the *Weltgeist* these seeds began to germinate in the idealism of Croce and Gentile.

Croce's theory of aesthetic intuition and Gentile's account of thinking as a dialectical process of self-criticism provide between them the foundation stones for Lombardi's account of "the individual who thinks." But he holds that both of them in different ways fell victim to the fear of freedom and personal responsibility from which the perennial allure of the theological conception of truth arises; and for this reason they forced their results back into the old metaphysical molds of the one universal World Spirit and the absolutely unique, transcendental and self-founding Ego.

I shall not here comment upon Lombardi's criticism of Croce, but I want to pause for a moment over what he regards as the fundamental "paralogism of Gentile": "without being aware that he is herein making a transition from a first to a second proposition, Gentile reasons from the validity of actual thinking to the absolute Thought of a World Spirit, just because behind the first proposition he immediately introduces his own opinion that only a metaphysically unique thought can be an absolutely valid thought." [20] Because of this, the "polygonic" or pluralistic character of actual experience (which Gentile himself emphasizes) remains without foundation in his theory: "Gentile can give an account only of the individuation that the World Spirit may achieve *in me* the speaker." [21] This "paralogism" is the one which English idealists were finding in Gentile at about the time that Lombardi was first isolating it in the twenties and thirties.[22] Roger Holmes faced it resolutely and identified one possible way of avoiding it when he charac-

20. *Nascita*, pp. 150-151.
21. *Ibid.*, p. 152.
22. See especially W. G. DeBurgh, "Gentile's Philosophy of the Spirit," *Philosophy*, IV (1929), 3-22; reprinted as Chapter 5 in *Towards A Religious Philosophy* (London, 1937). Compare my remarks about Bosanquet's attitude to actual idealism in G. Gentile, *Genesis and Structure of Society* (Urbana, 1960), pp. 11-13, 29.

terized Gentile's view as the attempt to develop a consistent
solipsism. But his proposed reform of Gentile's dialectic through
the complete elimination of the personal Ego bears out Lombardi's view that Gentile's theory of truth is ultimately *theological.*[23] I myself would say that Gentile had not perfectly
solved the problem in his *Logic* and that he often talks in a
way that makes the theological interpretation seem the only
possible one. And yet even in the *Logic* it is clear that Gentile
means to preserve the "polygonic" character of thought; and
I have set forth elsewhere my reasons for holding that he *did*
arrive at a satisfactory solution in his last book and that its
basic elements can be found in his *Logic* and even earlier.[24]
We shall see in a moment that it is a crux of Lombardi's
philosophy also.

As we saw, Lombardi finds the key for a really "modern"
philosophy in the initial recognition that there is no purely
contemplative neutral, rational thought; there is only an individual who thinks, a person with needs and concerns of his
own (some of which he may not be directly conscious of),
a man with a certain natural biological inheritance, and a certain
social environment. His consciousness is a focal point for all
of this as well as for his memories of past experience; and his
actual thinking is an attempt to bring all of it to bear on
some *decision* (*krisis*) that he has to make here and now in
his present situation. The decision is expressed in words, but
the thinking is a function of the critical self-consciousness that
produces the words (or perhaps I should say, it *is* the self-
consciousness).[25]

23. R. W. Holmes, *The Idealism of Giovanni Gentile* (New York,
1937), pp. 112 ff., 157 ff., 226-227.

24. The whole problem, and all of Gentile's successive attempts to solve
it, are discussed at some length in my *Social Philosophy of Giovanni
Gentile,* pp. 102-125, 251-284. For a critique of the "theological" interpretation of Gentile, see especially pp. 294-302.

25. This conception of thinking is expounded and developed in all of
Lombardi's books; see, for instance, as the immediate source of the
present account, *Nascita,* pp. 201- 208.

If we want to see as precisely as possible what thinking is, we must consider the tension involved in reaching forward from the word or words that are already formulated in our minds to the still unformulated content of what, speaking proleptically, we ordinarily call our "thought(s)." According to Lombardi's analysis, this involves a *tacit* self-critical awareness of a problem to be solved, a choice or decision to be made. We can see why he insists that consciousness is both self-critical and yet *tacit*, when we reflect on the fact that the completed thought embodied in words is only the *final product* of actual thinking. Lombardi's analysis is here clearly rooted in Gentile's distinction between *pensiero pensante* and *pensiero pensato;* but where Gentile saw simply a limit for verbal knowledge (one can never *define* the actual Ego), Lombardi finds the *opening* for a reintegration into human thought of all the aspects of experience—sensation, emotions, the dim awareness of organic functions, and even the psychological unconscious. Gentile himself used this "opening" in his theory of education and in his philosophy of art, but his attachment to the old logic of the rational absolute caused him to describe what he was doing in formulas that are as full of paradox as anything in Kierkegaard.[26]

I have no doubt that Lombardi has here found the right interpretation of Gentile's *pure act*, and a much clearer way of expressing it than Gentile ever found. But I must confess that —partly, no doubt, because of the extreme sketchiness of the discussion in *Nascita del mondo moderno* at this point—I find his account of what he calls "the profound intelligence of life"

26. Thus art is *non*-actual or unactual, although it is the living creative activity of the subject. Subjective feeling—though unactual—is God-in-us; while God is the "moment" of absolute *ob*jectivity and so is unactual for that quite opposite reason. Pain is not actual, and so on. I shall not extend the list to include what Gentile says about evil and error, for I think that on these topics Gentile's view is not viciously paradoxical. The paradoxes about the "past" character of evil and error are manufactured by critical misunderstandings, and a right understanding of these cases provides the key for a reformulation of the others in ways that are not so directly insulting to the intellect.

the most cryptic part of his doctrine.[27] Fairly clearly he wants to bridge the gulf between historical idealism and evolutionary naturalism: human history is to be restored to the context of natural history. This seems to me eminently sensible and a great improvement on the rigidity of Croce's refusal to recognize that since Darwin "natural history" really has been a historical discipline.[28]

Something like the same doctrine of a *tacit* self-consciousness is, I think, to be found in Sartre's doctrine of pre-reflective consciousness. But in Sartre I cannot find anything at this level corresponding to the self-critical function that is so important in Lombardi's theory; and I think it is for this reason that I find Sartre's account of the freedom to which we are "condemned" so unsatisfactory. In Lombardi's view the thought that results from the settling or decision of a present problem must be called superficial or profound according to the measure of its success as a critical self-expression. Every thought is a *concept* insofar as the whole complex of the individual's experience is somehow grasped by it or contained in it; and the self-expression is itself *critical* insofar as it leads to further thoughts, because of the explicit recognition of difficulties and objections stimulated in the process of its formulation.[29]

This self-critical aspect of my own thought is of crucial importance in my communication with others. I understand others by virtue of the same self-conscious critical activity through which I understand myself. But *my* self-conscious

27. *Nascita*, pp. 208-209. The fuller account, to which his footnote there refers, is in a mimeographed handbook for his students and is not generally available.

28. But, in a spirit of Puckish mischief, I cannot help remarking that when Lombardi says that "the life of the species in us, or rather the species that we are . . . knows many things better than we do" (*Nascita*, p. 209), he is far closer to Hegel's *Naturphilosophie*, for which in general he has only harsh words, than any Italian Hegelian since Spaventa has dared or even wanted to come.

29. *Nascita*, pp. 201-208. Gentile's theory of the concept as *self*-concept is in the background here.

criticism remains mine and is not identical with the self-conscious criticism by which others understand me. Thus no metaphysically unique thinking or self is anywhere involved.

Similarly this critical self-expression in its varying degrees is the actuality of freedom. Human freedom or liberty is not the absolute essence of a purely spiritual activity, but the gathering of all one's energies into the decision of the theoretical or practical question with which one is at a given moment faced. Liberty is "burdensome" (*pesante*) because it is the acceptance of a burden.[30]

Finally, this purely human conception of thinking allows us to give a satisfactory account of truth and error. When I think —when I think philosophically, that is—I strive to make the whole of my experience coherent, and when I have done my best I call the results *true*. But in virtue of my tacit critical self-consciousness, I always know as part of my truth that there are unresolved difficulties and gaps which only the experience of others can fill. Thus I know that many things which I take to be true provisionally may turn out to be errors; furthermore I recognize that truth is a social and not a private possession. Unless I am here mistaken (and I am indeed critically conscious at this point that I may be), Lombardi's conception of truth is very close to, perhaps identical with, Peirce's ideal consensus of an infinite community of investigators.[31]

In its own context, however, Lombardi's conception of truth as a social construction of solutions for the common problems of the world of men takes us back to the problem of the polygonic character of truth and the supposed "paralogism" of Gentile. Gentile, it should be remembered, insisted from the beginning that the transcendental Ego never completely exists, it is always *in fieri*, in the process of becoming; and in

30. *Ibid.*, pp. 210-211; for a full account, see *Il concetto della libertà* (Asti, 1955; now Rome).

31. Professor Lombardi has now confirmed this interpretation. But since my uncertainty was genuine I have allowed the parenthesis to stand because of its paradigmatic value.

his final account this process became an explicitly social dialogue between the self and its own other, and more particularly
between the soul and the body, between sense and reason.[32]
I now wish to suggest that Lombardi cannot afford to dispense
with the transcendental Ego in the two opposite capacities of
real foundation of personal individuality and *ideal aim* of
community life.

About its functioning as a real foundation for individuality
I think the only possible quarrel between Lombardi and myself
would be merely verbal. His conception of "the profound
intelligence of life" seems to be an empirical counterpart of
the Ego; and when he speaks of the modern revolution as
involving "a new sense of the sociality of man, and the solidarity of humanity in every single individual" he must mean at
least as much as I mean by the transcendental Ego as *real
foundation* and probably some part of what I refer to as *ideal
aim.* But I rather suspect he would say that the present divided
state of the world is an object lesson against making an absolute out of the *aims* of any community whatsoever; and I for
my part would agree that in an era where communities with
age-old traditions, developed in isolation, are being forced out
of their isolation into active co-existence, the solidarity of the
biological species, the community of basic economic needs,
is probably the most reliable basis for communication. The
point I would urge is that although we must and should *begin*
here, we cannot stop at this. We have to work for a world
community of the so-called "higher" values, precisely because
otherwise the conflicts between lesser communities over these
values will continually undo whatever foundation of trust and
mutual understanding is successfully laid at the economic level.

But why call this sort of community "Ego"? From Lombardi's point of view at least, I think I can answer this question,
though I would not claim that I can persuade everyone else.
The answer is that this is the only way to reconcile the claim

32. See *Genesis and Structure of Society*, Chapters 4-13.

that *thinking* is always *personal* ("There is no thought; there is only an individual who thinks.") with the admission that *truth* is *social*. The "paralogism" of which Gentile is accused (rightly or wrongly and regardless of whether or not it is a paralogism) certainly involves a mistaken point of view. We must not argue, "My actual thought can be absolutely true, if and only if it is really the thought of a unique world spirit." [33] We must not argue in this way because it does not get us anywhere except into a metaphysical game which is as useless as it is, in my opinion, harmless. We must rather recognize that "I can only claim that my actual thought is true if I am willing to submit it for criticism at least by anyone whom I regard as a person of good will"; and in this case the crucial problem becomes how can I be sure that I have *truly* communicated my thought, or *rightly* interpreted the other's criticism. If we take Lombardi at his word we should have to say that there is no sense in the adverbs "truly" and "rightly" here, because he often seems to imply that there is no sense in which I and my neighbor either do or can have the same thought. The other man's thinking is his thinking and mine is mine (and therefore, although we use words like "community," "sociality," and "solidarity," we never really have anything *in common;* for certainly if we cannot share our thoughts we cannot share anything else, or at least can never *know* that we share it). By arguing in this way from his more polemical utterances we could show that Lombardi must agree with Kierkegaard not merely in his starting point—"the individual who thinks," but also in his conclusion—"the truth that is subjectivity." But since no conclusion could possibly be more abhorrent to him, it is clear that we must admit truth as a common possession and a unifying ideal. And since we cannot

33. In passing let me say that as long as the word "absolutely" is stressed, I cannot see any *danger* in this assertion and hence I myself would hesitate to call it a paralogism: no one ever can in fact *know* that his actual thought is the absolute or "theological" truth.

conceive this human *ideal* in the purely objective or *theological* mode of Plato's theory of Forms, the transcendental Ego, though driven from the door with maledictions, slips in again at the unprotected window. To illustrate, let us take one of the cases where Gentile himself seems to me to have failed, the case of pain (which is surely a *private* experience if any experience is private).

It is (in some sense of the word) a *logical* fact that I cannot *have* my neighbor's toothache; but it is also a *biological* fact that I do myself get toothache (or at least other bodily aches), and hence anything that my neighbor can intelligibly say to himself about his toothache he can also say to me and I can understand him. Furthermore, I can sympathize with him actively in the sense of helping him to do something about it. Generally I am in a better position to do something about it than he is precisely because I do not literally or passively sympathize, because I do not share the pain. But if I am to sympathize actively, we must share not merely a theoretical understanding of the problem but a practical attitude as well: we must have a common *aim*. If I do share his practical attitude (that is, if I follow the command of Christian charity and seek to love him as myself), a real community begins to exist between us so far as our actions are directed toward the solution of the common problem. That his problem really is my problem I can show only by my experimental solicitude in dealing with it. Because the pain is absolutely private, and often, as in the case of toothache, almost intractable without special knowledge and equipment, community in this particular case is probably harder to establish than in any other, and the sufferers of physical pain are notoriously cynical about the expressed sympathy of their would-be comforters. But when and if the pain begins to yield to treatment they have no trouble in believing in the sympathy.

The theoretical structure of common concepts through which I can understand and at least partially share even my neighbor's most private experiences—for if he can talk about it at all, even to himself, there must be some level of conceptual abstraction at which I can truthfully say I have had an experience "of the same type"—is what is meant by the transcendental Ego on the theoretical side. It is transcendental for both of us in whatever sense the conceptual structure is *common* or in whatever sense people share *the same* thoughts. What analysis of "common" or "same" is to be given here is a question of technical epistemology about which I think we can afford to be absolutely indifferent unless and until it emerges that people who give one analysis have a tendency to *act* differently towards their fellows from those who give another. Then and only then shall we be able to judge whether there is a significant *human* (not just a metaphysical, or, I am tempted to say, merely verbal) difference between their theories. It is the *practical* reality of the transcendental Ego that matters. And in one sense, though not in his technically defined sense, Lombardi is quite right about its *theological* character.

The Ego of the "pure act" is the Christian God *in whose love* we must love our neighbors as ourselves.[34] But it is a God who exists *in us* and depends absolutely *upon us*, a God of this world of men only, and a charity of finite human individuals one to another. In our practical relations this unity in God exists so far as we can actually find ways of settling disputes which all parties regard as fair and solutions which all parties accept as just. All this "treating," "regarding," and "accepting," moreover, must take place as far as possible in the medium of free rational criticism. Hence it is not merely violence and coercion in the sense of physical pain (the abso-

34. It is interesting to note that Ugo Spirito who reacted like Lombardi against the seeming dogmatism of Gentile's *Logic* has ended by rediscovering this truth about Gentile's absolute; but I think that, unlike Lombardi, he cast away too much in his flight from Gentile and cannot any longer regain a firm footing, but must remain suspended uneasily between the skepticism of *La vita come ricerca* and the mysticism of *La vita come amore.*

lutely private experience) that is to be avoided, but violence in the technical sense defined by Collingwood—i.e., any governance of men through appeals to their passions and emotions (all of which are similarly private).[35] The transcendental Ego is the ideal of a life that is shared as fully as possible, and it is very simply and easily distinguished from the empirical ego of each one of us, which is the private, unshareable aspect of our experience.

Gentile became a Fascist and hence the theologian (as Lombardi would put it) of a truth that existed only in a future state which he constructed in his imagination. But because of the interdependence of the philosophical concepts of truth and freedom—which Lombardi has rightly emphasized—there is no truth that *cannot* be perverted in this way; and because of the burdensome character of freedom itself, there is no truth that *is* not. Even the biological solidarity in which Lombardi puts his faith is perverted into racialism, which is probably the worst of all the "theologies" we have so far been offered. We must realize, therefore, that when Hegel identified the spirit of modern philosophy as the spirit of Christianity he was not thinking of the spirit of the Crusades or of the Inquisition, but of the spirit of charity translated into purely human terms.[36]

35. *The New Leviathan* (Oxford, 1942), 20.5-20.59.
36. One can see this by studying Hegel's early essay which Nohl titles "The Spirit of Christianity and its Fate," and then examining *his* account of the "birth of the modern world" in the *Phenomenology:* We leave the "unhappy consciousness" of Judaism and medieval Christianity behind us as we enter "the daylight of the present"; and at first the values that concern us are just the values of the secular Renaissance and Enlightenment to which Lombardi gives prominence. When we reach the Romantics we rise for the first time to the full conception of Spirit, and this sends us straight back to the ancient world; we come back again to the Enlightenment, but this time viewed as a conflict of religious and secular elements. The French Revolution shows us the triumph of secular reason and its ruin, and it is only with Hegel's own humanist reinterpretation and reintegration of Kantian moral philosophy with the Christian ideal of charity (in the section called "evil and forgiveness") that the *modern spirit* at last achieves a stable form.

It is just because I agree (I think) with Lombardi's conception of human thinking, and (certainly) with his conception of human freedom; just because I recognize therefore that any truth is double-edged, capable of a lazy, bigoted trust-in-God-and-our-reward-in-the-next-world interpretation as well as a properly human and responsible one—it is precisely for these reasons that, in spite of the many insights I have gained from Lombardi's works, and the many dangers I am grateful to have been alerted against, I remain unrepentantly wedded both to the Gentilian concept of the transcendental Ego and to the Hegelian thesis that the spirit of the modern world is the spirit of Christianity.

BIBLIOGRAPHY OF THE PRINCIPAL WRITINGS OF FRANCO LOMBARDI

L'Esperienza e l'uomo: Fondamenti di una filosofia umanistica, Florence, 1935.

Il mondo degli uomini, Florence, 1935.

Ludovico Feuerbach: Seguito da una scelta di passi tradotti, Florence, 1935.

Kierkegaard, Florence, 1936.

La libertà del volere e l'individuo, Milan, 1941.

(NOTE: Publication of this book was gravely hindered by the war and not many copies were circulated.)

Nascita del mondo moderno, Asti, 1953.

(NOTE: This and all the volumes which follow in this Bibliography, except *Il piano del nostro sapere*, have been published since 1960 by the Istituto di filosofia dell'Università di Roma.)

—Translated into French by G. Bufo, *Naissance du monde moderne*, Paris, 1958.

—Translated into German by W. Eike, *Die Geburt der modernen Welt*, Cologne, 1960.

(NOTE: An English translation was apparently planned by the "World Institute of Culture" in Bangalore in 1958, but has not yet appeared.)

Concetto e problemi della storia della filosofia, Asti, 1954; now Rome.

Il concetto della libertà, Asti, 1955. (First published in Rome, 1947, and since 1960 by the Istituto di filosofia dell'Università.)

Dopo lo storicismo, Asti, 1955; now Rome.

Ricostruzione filosofica, Asti, 1956; now Rome.

—Anonymous English translation in *Mankind* (India), No. 10 (1960), pp. 18-31 and No. 11 (1960), pp. 40-59.

Il piano del nostro sapere, Rome, 1958.

La filosofia italiana negli ultimi cento anni, Asti, 1958; now Rome.

La posizione dell'uomo nell'universo, Florence (for the Istituto di filosofia dell'Università di Roma), 1963.

(NOTE: This is the first volume of a new edition of Lombardi's writings. It was published too recently to be available for consultation during the revision of my essay for the press. This book, together with his articles in the new journal *De Homine* —Rome, Centro di ricerca per le scienze morali e sociali and Istituto di filosofia dell'Università, 1962 et seq.—of which he is the founder and editor, provides the latest statement of Lombardi's position and in his own view marks a new stage in the evolution of his thought.)

EUGENE F. KAELIN

Three Stages on Sartre's Way

AN ESSAY IN CONTEMPORARY FRENCH PHILOSOPHY

I

When, in 1950, a group of French and American philosophers were asked to pool their knowledge in the production of a series of essays that were to represent "the major trends in contemporary French and American philosophy," the volume which resulted was published here as *Philosophic Thought in France and the United States.*[1] In France, the same work appeared in two volumes, and was called *L'activité philosophique contemporaine en France et aux États-Unis.* In all, eighteen essays purported to give the essence of contemporary French philosophy; and an overview was supplied by Professor Richard McKeon in a supplementary essay entitled "An American Reaction to the Present Situation in French Philosophy."[2]

1. Edited by Professor Marvin Farber (Buffalo, 1950).
2. *Ibid.*, pp. 337-362.

Two of these essays will concern us here. In his "The Present Situation and the Present Future of French Philosophy," [3] Jean Wahl noted ". . . that [the] intellectual youth in France seems to be divided into three parties: the Catholic, the Communist, and the existentialist." [4] And in Professor McKeon's overview we find the following suggestive image:

> The French philosophy which appears from this juxtaposition of eighteen essays can be conceived best on the analogy to a soft polygon . . . which changes its shape as it is set on various faces: some of the apices and faces can be distinguished, though distorted, in all positions of the polygon; some which are prominent when the polygon is in one position disappear entirely when it comes to rest on another face; sizes change, forms that were similar become incongruent, and lines that were parallel intersect.[5]

In my own effort to present one perspective on the contemporary French philosophical scene I shall concentrate on one "face" of the polygon, in an endeavor to show that it is, so to speak, a straight line; it is my hope that its clear delineation will enable other historians of the present to construct the other sides, and still others to perceive the forms which these sides determine as they relate to each other in the more conclusive configuration.

I propose to establish my line of the "soft polygon" by commenting upon Professor Wahl's tri-partite division of the intellectual youth of Gaul during the late forties and early fifties. Instead of referring to the three parties as "Catholic," "Communist," and "existentialist," I shall use the terms, which I take to be more accurate, "neo-scholastic," "Marxist," and "existentialist."

It is interesting, at the outset, to note that the division is thought to apply to the "philosophical youth," and not to the

3. *Ibid.*, pp. 35-54.
4. *Ibid.*, p. 38.
5. *Ibid.*, p. 340.

professional or academic philosophers of the period in question; for immediately we are made aware of the distinction between academic and non-academic philosophy. The academics were, for the most part, dedicated to the program of instruction leading to degrees, while the students, again for the most part, tended to take the academic program with a grain or two of salt and looked upon philosophy as a guide to the solution of life's problems, in particular those of social and political action. Where the teachers' studies were undertaken to rival the waning influence of the former generation, dominated by the so-called three B's of French philosophy (Bergson, Blondel and Brunschvicg), the students found solutions to the problems of their daily lives in the religious orientation of the scholastics, the social struggle of the Marxists, and the moral involvement which existentialists have found necessary to give meaning to their agonizing apprehension of personal freedom and universal responsibility.

In a word, while the teachers addressed themselves to the students' intellects, the latter were receiving a more "meaningful" message on another frequency, to which they responded with their whole personalities. This wide-spread influence of non-academic and value-toned philosophy on the culture of the nation is almost unknown in America, where, outside of the brief flare of pragmatism and a momentary dominance in American philosophy of social and political thinkers in the academy itself during the great depression, the values expressed in community living seldom achieve the light of philosophical reflection; instead, they remain implicit in the platforms of political parties, the programs of governmental administrations, and the activities of various religious and non-religious pressure groups. It is no wonder, then, that Europeans consider Americans as politically uninformed; in the main, our philosophers have abdicated an important social function. It is precisely this function that has been served by the non-academic philosophies of France.

Since 1950, when Professor Wahl's essay was published, a great many changes have occurred in French philosophy. In ten years' time, the youth has grown older, if it has not matured; and some of the then younger generation are now themselves dedicated to the academic program. Phenomenology is perhaps still the dominant academic philosophy; and neo-scholasticism is backed by the institutional structure of the Church, while most Marxist publications bear the imprimatur of the Communist Party. Existentialism, founded as a protest by Kierkegaard and Nietzsche to the overbearing rationality of Hegelian idealism, and continued in the works of Heidegger and Sartre, continues to put a premium on individual decision and personal responsibility, and seems, at least on the face of it, to be inimical to any organized form of social or institutional approbation. Moreover, the removal of Gilson and Maritain to the North American continent has greatly weakened the cause of French neo-scholasticism, and the quasi-official attitude of anti-clericalism tends to offset any advantage which neo-scholasticism may have drawn from the Church's support. The two philosophies dominating French intellectual life today, then, are Marxism and existentialism. Jean-Paul Sartre has been trying very hard to be exemplary of both.

It is my purpose to trace out a sketch of Sartre's philosophical career from its academic beginnings (*L'Imagination*) through three gradually distinct phases: (1) the phenomenological (*L'Imaginaire; L'Être et le néant*); (2) the politically polemical (*Matérialisme et révolution; Les communistes et la paix*); and (3) the critically Marxist (*Questions de méthode; Critique de la raison dialectique*). If all goes well with Sartre's own plans, his career will culminate in a forthcoming tome on the philosophy of history, the proposed second volume of his massive *Critique*.[6]

6. *Critique de la raison dialectique* (Paris, 1960).

II

Sartre's own attitude toward the education he had received at the *École Normale Supérieure*, as well as that toward the philosophy he himself professed at Le Havre before his sojourn in Berlin in 1933-34 (at the *Institut Français*), may best be summed up in the following quotation:

> We have all read Brunschvicg, Lalande and Meyerson: we have all been led to believe that the mind, like a giant spider, attracted things into its web, covered them over with its white spittle and slowly deglutinated them, thereby reducing them to its own substance.[7]

In exchange for the idealism of the reigning French masters, Sartre was willing to accept the influence of the Germans: Husserl, Scheler, Heidegger, and Jaspers, with whose work he became acquainted during his year's tenure at Berlin. The notion of "intentionality," he believed, would permit philosophers to empty consciousness of matter at the same time that matter was left to be conceived as it is in-itself, unmoved by any mind—as simple external relatedness. In terms of the dialectic he was to adopt later, he might have said that the materialism of d'Holbach and Helvétius met its antithesis in the idealism of a later period, and the two were to be synthesized in the phenomenological axiom, "Every consciousness is a consciousness of something." [8] In every act of awareness, whether intellectual or emotional, consciousness and its object are given simultaneously. Sartre's philosophy has never lost the tinge of this metaphysical dualism.

His first philosophical study was published in 1936, and bears all the marks of an academic treatise. It should be remembered that Sartre was at the time still teaching philosophy at a lycée

7. Sartre, "Une idée fondamentale de la 'Phénoménologie' de Husserl, l'intentionnalité," *Nouvelle Revue Française*, 52 (1939), 129.

8. See *L'Être et le néant* (Paris, 1943), "La preuve ontologique," p. 27.

in Le Havre, which was to become *Bouville* (the "city of mud") in his novel, *La Nausée*. I mention the novel for a reason which has often been neglected in studies of Sartre's career. The title of that first treatise is *L'Imagination*, and the treatise itself is an attempt to show that the classical formulations of the "mental" image are based upon a loose analogy with "material" images, or signs, and that in consequence both rationalists and empiricists have been dupes of "the illusion of immanence," the mistaken notion that what is seen in an image is a content of consciousness. What Sartre was looking for and could not find was a rational explanation of a primary datum of his experience: as he would put it, human freedom, which expresses itself in the literary artist's ability to imagine the universe other than it is perceived to be.

According to Alain, whose aesthetic theory was enjoying unprecedented vogue among French intellectuals, the difference between a veridical perception and an image was an error in the subject's judgment of what is given by the senses. But Alain's aesthetics was built upon a strictly physiological psychology, which denied the existence of mental images as such. According to Sartre, a theory of the imagination which denies the existence of images leaves something to be desired. Finally, what was ultimately desired Sartre found in Husserl's phenomenology.

Sartre accepted Husserl's distinction between perception and imagination as two kinds of mental acts: the first is a passive synthesis, while the second is an active expression, or spontaneous act. In other words, the difference lies in the intentional structures of the various acts. Noting that Husserl's discussion of the "imaging" consciousness includes a reference to matter and form, that the matter of a physical image is given to perception while that of the mental image is not, Sartre proposed a modification of Husserl's system. He granted the intentional difference in the structures of perceptual and imaginative acts;

as he put it, the distinction is necessary, but not sufficient for a coherent theory of the imagination. What was lacking was a thorough-going phenomenological description of the various kinds of images. And at that point Sartre's independent career began. His first original treatise bears the title *L'Imaginaire*. We enter here upon the first of the three stages I have indicated.

(1) *The phenomenological period.* Having defined "consciousness," in his first treatise, as spontaneous activity [9] outwardly directed toward an environing world, Sartre shows, in the second, how images may be classified according to an increasing order of spontaneity in the mental act involved. He arranges the "family" of images in the following ascending order: (1) portraits and caricatures; (2) signs (plaques, etc.); (3) mimic gestures; (4) abstract designs (two-dimensional representations of three-dimensional realities); (5) illusory phenomena (faces in flames, spots on walls, human shapes in natural forms); (6) hypnagogical images; (7) mental images per se. The gradation in spontaneity is described in terms of an abstraction from the "matter" of the image which is formed by the intention of the act.

Having "bracketed the world" in order to intuit the essence of the experience, Sartre describes that essence in the following definition: an image is "an act which, in its corporeity, aims at an absent or inexistent object by means of a physical or psychical continuant which is not given in itself, but [which is given] in the guise of an 'analogical representative' of the object aimed at." [10] Insofar as it is the referent of a mental act, the object of an image is always given "in absence," i.e., it is in some respect "unreal." The conclusion of Sartre's phenomenological psychology of the imagination contains a discussion of "the aesthetic object," which utilizes this "essential description" of images, and outlines a theory of aesthetics that

9. *L'Imagination* (Paris, 1936), pp. 1-3.
10. *L'Imaginaire* (Paris, 1940), p. 75.

could be completed should aestheticians take the time to correlate this text with Sartre's other aesthetic writings: primarily his criticism, his "existential psycho-analyses" of authors, and his literary manifesto.

L'Être et le néant, Sartre's phenomenological ontology, was called for by the conclusions of *L'Imaginaire*. What does it mean to say that the objects of images are "unreal objects"? In order to formulate his answer to this question, Sartre made use of the dualism which he had already marked out in *L'Imagination* between consciousness and its objects. The one exists for itself, and is nothing without its correlate, which exists in itself, since an unconscious consciousness is a flat self-contradiction. Whereas the "being of phenomena" is measured by the fact that something appears to some consciousness, the "phenomenon of being" can be experienced only by virtue of a special emotional access: in Heidegger's case, this access was supplied by boredom (*Langweile*); and in Sartre's, by nausea. The special emotional access to the negation of being for both these men derives from Kierkegaard's notion of dread; for Heidegger it is *Angst*, and for Sartre, *angoisse*. The shift in Sartre's philosophy from the influence of Husserl to that of Heidegger follows the level of abstraction indicated by the distinction between the being of phenomena and the phenomenon of being.

A note here on the Heideggerian influence: the German's incomprehensible "*Das Nichts nichtet*," becomes in Sartre's more understandable French, "*Le néant se néantise*." Neither *nichten* nor *se néantiser* occurs in the dictionaries of the respective common languages; they were coined to indicate the relation between Being and its negation. But the intransitive or absolute sense of *nichten* makes nonsense of the meaning intended in the German, whereas the reflexive verb used by Sartre permits translation into the passive voice, so that the expression may be rendered "Nothingness is nihilated." The relation of nihilation is described in terms of an "internal negation," and this expression in its turn is explicated by analogy with the perceptual experience of an optical illusion. Thus, in terms of the Gestaltist interpretation of such illusions, two elements, the figure and the ground, are "internally and negatively" related in a perceptual field. If what is initially the figure of the perception switches its position in the field and becomes the ground, what was the ground becomes the figure, and a new "object" is seen. Consciousness and its object, the for-itself and the in-itself, are like figure and ground: we can become aware of the one only at the expense of an awareness of the other (due regard being given to the differences between a "positional" (*thétique*) and "non-positional" awareness). The nothingness which is consciousness is nihilated by an awareness of the being of the world. A fuller awareness of one's own nothingness may be had in every situation in which the person must decide to act in such a way as to realize one of his own "real possibilities," offered by the objective structure of the situation itself.

Besides affording an insight into what has come to be called Sartre's "theater of situations," the anguish of decision gives further insight into Sartre's distrust of Marxist determinism. Following the publication of *Les Mains Sales*, one Communist called its author "a gravedigger," and another insisted that existentialism is not a humanism.[11] To the one he replied that he would rather be a grave-digger who works for himself than a lackey who works for another; and to the other, that the denial of a universal human nature is not tantamount to a denial of humanism, if only one permitted oneself to *think* about the matter. Be that as it may, two outstanding difficulties arose from this early argument with contemporary Marxists, who

11. In answer to Sartre's *L'Existentialisme est un humanisme* (Paris, 1946). See Jean Kanapa, *L'Existentialisme n'est pas un humanisme* (Paris, 1947).

were all too eager to point out Sartre's supposed "individualism" (read "solipsism") and "pessimism."

The basis for the charge of pessimism is to be found in the conclusion of Sartre's discussion of human "ambiguity," viz., "Man is a useless passion." But man is a useless passion in Sartre's scheme only because he insists upon being like God, i.e., a being existing for-itself-in-itself, which is a logical absurdity. Sartre has inverted St. Anselm's proof by stating that God is that being whose essence implies his non-existence. Man's passion is not useless when it is expended in an effort to change the character of the universe to coincide more closely with man's own desires. And this effort is of the essence of Marxist "humanism."

In answer to the second charge, that his earlier philosophy is solipsistic, Sartre could refer to his foreknowledge that existentialism navigates very close to the "reef of solipsism," and to the fact that his analysis of shame was intended to avoid that reef. The fact that it fails to do so will not concern us here. It could be further pointed out that the mode of being a subject with others is already sketched out, in *L'Être*, as an analysis of the situation of work. But unsympathetic readers of *Huis Clos* who light upon Garcin's statement that "Hell is other people," deduce therefrom a misanthropic strain in Sartre's thought, and thereby miss the intent of the remark, which was to indicate the manner in which a human being can, in "bad faith," assume an essence by accepting the determination of others. To assume an essence which results from the action of others is to become a "transcendence transcended," i.e., organized into the significant universe of another transcendence, of another conscious human being. The Communists were right to insist, however, that the struggle of transcendences is the fundamental relationship between two consciousnesses, as Sartre depicted that relationship in *L'Être;* even so, no one is better situated than the members of the proletarian class within "bourgeois" society to know what it means to have one's means of development cut off in the face of another, transcendent class. This movement from the individualism of the person to the "socialism" of the class is the key to Sartre's later development.

(2) *Literature and politics.* The second stage on Sartre's way,[12] is a transitional period between the predominantly individualistic and psychological phase we have just synopsized and the later, Marxist, period, in which Sartre's emphasis shifts to the more social aspects of man's being-in-the-world. He followed the publication of *L'Être* with other works in which his ontology is used primarily as a structural device, and gave three notable examples of the manner in which his "existential psychoanalysis" could be carried out: first, in an analysis of the "structures" of anti-semitic behavior in *Réflexions sur la question juive*, and later in the studies of the lives and works of Baudelaire and Jean Genêt.

The distinctive mark of this second stage is chiefly its polemical character. In *Qu'est-ce que la littérature?* Sartre argued for a new conception of the role of the literary artist as a political agent. He proposed the term "total literature" to cover his ideal notion, which was to complete the partial objectives found in "bourgeois" and "proletarian" letters, known respectively by four differentiating categories: (1) dominant metaphysical points of view (being vs. doing); (2) historical emphases (*hexis* vs. *praxis*); (3) purposes (enjoyment vs. exposure); and (4) techniques (analysis vs. synthesis). For our present purposes, the interesting categories are to be found in the apparently parallel formulations of metaphysics and history. Some light may be thrown on the distinctions involved

12. The title of this essay is foreshadowed by the literary analyses of Robert Champigny, in *Stages on Sartre's Way* (Bloomington, 1959). The author of this literary study does not intend to indicate Sartre's debt to Kierkegaard, as does the present writer.

if we recall Sartre's claim, in *L'Être*, that the human being has no existence, no *être*, outside of what it does, its *praxis*.[13] Further, it must be noted that in order to act one must do something within the bounds of two limits: the present situation in which one finds oneself and a projected end which is the goal of the activity itself. Being and doing, *hexis* and *praxis*, are thus synthesized into the single concept of intentionality.

In a second series of articles appearing in this polemical period (*Matérialisme et révolution*), Sartre begins to emphasize the notion of *praxis* as a substitute for that of intentionality.[14] Metaphysically considered, however, the difference is not great; in Sartre's description, the worker's freedom in action still sounds like literary creation:

> What he [a worker] becomes aware of, in the course of the action itself, is that he surpasses the present state of matter by a precise plan of disposing it in such or such a way; and since this plan is nothing but the arrangement of means in view of ends, he succeeds in fact in redisposing it as he has wished.[15]

But, even in the case of the worker, the matter to be redisposed need not be physical, since the worker's situation is not primarily a purely physical concept. In viewing the situation of the practical agent, the "revolutionary" philosopher

> . . . sees human relations from the point of view of work, work being his lot. But work is, among other things, a direct relation of man with the universe—the "hold" man has on nature—and, at the same time, a primitive type of relation between men.[16]

13. *L'Être et le néant*, pp. 555 ff.
14. This shift in emphasis is necessitated by Sartre's growing social consciousness. The moral connotation involved has been developed, through an examination of Sartre's literary productions, by Champigny, *op. cit.*
15. This article has been re-published in *Situations III* (Paris, 1949). My translation of the text, p. 204.
16. *Ibid.*, p. 180.

We recognize, of course, the accepted Marxian doctrine that man's relation to man is determined by men's reciprocal relations arising from their individual "mediating" relationship to machines, the means of production in a capitalist economy. The revolutionary philosopher, however, is no mere social agitator. Unlike the social reformers who argue for the civil rights of negroes and Jews in the name of a universal human nature, and who would "integrate" the oppressed peoples into the existing social structure, Sartre insists that philosophy must be put to work to change the social structure itself, since it is that structure which determines one's rights.

What can be said, then, of those members of the French "working class" who on June 4, 1952, refused to engage in the general strike against the government, ordered by the Communist party, in retaliation for its having, by force of police arms, broken up a Communist demonstration in Paris on May 28th of the same year? A third series of articles in Sartre's second phase (*Les communistes et la paix*) was dedicated to finding an answer to this question.

In it Sartre declared himself a Communist sympathizer, but insisted upon using his own principles for resolving his differences with the party. For his pains, he was condemned as a "revisionist" and an "intellectual flatfoot" (*flic-intellectuel*).[17] Jean Kanapa, the Communist responsible for this treatment, wanted a "proletarian class" made up of workers, and not of renegade petit-bourgeois writers. Sartre's statement that a proletarian class could exist only in act as it works out its social objectives did not jibe with another, that "The ideal would be that the proletariat be pure relation, that which arises wherever two workers are together." [18] So, it will be remem-

17. The epithet is used by Jean Kanapa in an article in *L'Humanité*, February 22, 1954.

18. Sartre, "Les communistes et la paix (II)," *Les Temps Modernes*, 8^1 (1952), 761.

bered, was to be the Church of Christ. The third of this series
of articles sought out the facts describing the French economic
scene, which would explain the proletariat's dilatory tactics.
Following his rejection by the orthodox Communists, Sartre
published a special issue of *Les Temps Modernes*, dedicated to
a description of the political Left, in May, 1955. The lead
article, "Rightist Thinking Today" ("La Pensée de droite,
aujourd'hui"), was supplied by Simone de Beauvoir.

Sartre has been criticized by men of the right for his "na-
ïveté": classes, they claim, do not exist outside of a more general social structure in which each is synthesized. The individual *hexis* and the social *praxis* cannot be defined in the same
way, at least not without a description of the social dynamics,
according to which men form groups and groups determine
individual behavior. Merleau-Ponty, a former member of Sartre's group of "mandarins," according to whom the idea of
dialectic has been degraded into sheer ideology,[19] criticized
Sartre for his "naïve" theory of history (which has not yet
been developed in detail), as well as for his self-deluding idea
that literature can be a political act.[20] We have already shown
that the worker's freedom has been conceived on the basis
of an analogy with the literary artist's imaginative activity.
As Merleau-Ponty has put it, to conceive of literature as a
political act is a personal decision of the writer to stay within
the realm of the imaginary. In this sense Merleau-Ponty attempts to show that in committing literature to politics Sartre
has "unwittingly" committed politics to literature.

(3) *Critical Marxism*. Sartre's third and final stage is composed of works which were calculated to answer his critics,
both from the Right and from the Left. The first work of
this period was *Questions de méthode*, published in *Les Temps*

19. See his *Les aventures de la dialectique* (Paris, 1955), which includes
an essay entitled "Sartre et l'ultra-bolchevisme," pp. 131-271.
20. *Ibid.*, p. 271.

Modernes in 1957. It had been composed at the behest of the Polish review, *Twórczość*, whose editors requested an article from Sartre on "The Situation of Existentialism in 1957." The same article appears as the first part of the *Critique de la raison dialectique* (1960).

Rightists are condemned for their "bourgeois" thought, which turns out to be nothing more than the method of analysis, or the reduction of the complex phenomenon to be explained into its simple constituent elements. If the analytical method may be said to work in the sciences, it does so only because of the degree of abstraction permitted to the methods of mathematics and physics. "American sociologists," whom Sartre cites as exemplary bourgeois thinkers, use the analytic method in the field of social relations without due regard to the concrete situations in which those relations are generated. His opponents on the Left are goaded for their sterile materialism in the realm of theory, and for their method of terrorism (elimination of dissidents) in the realm of practice. As a means of avoiding the abstraction of analysis, Sartre adopts the method of the French Marxist, Henri Lefèbvre (who was expelled from the French Communist party as a "revisionist" in 1958).

This method, called by Sartre "progressive-regressive," has three components: (1) the descriptive (observation informed by a valid general theory); (2) the analytico-regressive (ordering phenomena in a temporal sequence); and (3) the historico-genetic (study of the process of development; elucidation and explanation of the present in terms of the general historical enterprise itself).[21] Sartre's aim in adopting Lefèbvre's method is to facilitate the development of a Marxist theory of knowledge.

Knowledge in this scheme is inevitably linked with action:

A flight and a jump forward, both a refusal and a realization, a *project* retains and reveals the surpassed reality which

21. *Critique de la raison dialectique*, p. 42.

is rejected by the very movement that surpasses it: thus knowledge is an element of *praxis*, even its most rudimentary element; but that knowledge has nothing in common with an absolute awareness [*Savoir*]. Defined by the negation of the rejected reality in favor of a future to be produced, knowledge remains a captive of action and disappears with it.[22]

In order for a person not engaged in the activity in question to become aware of the dialectic of a particular social action, he must use a device which Sartre calls *compréhension*—translating the more usual German term *Verstehen*. In his elucidation of this method he repeats what he has already told us in "existential psychoanalysis"—that a project must be understood in terms of a present situation and a predicted future goal.

The most embarrassing doctrines of the orthodox Marxist position to be reconciled in a more inclusive view of dialectical reasoning are those of materialism and universal determinism. Sartre's *Critique*, which is supposed to do for dialectical reasoning what Kant's *Kritik* does for the scientific method—establish the conditions of its possibility and the limits of its acceptability—must therefore be re-interpreted if Sartre is to fulfill his rôle as Marxian ideologist.[23] The easier of the two concepts to be reformulated is that of matter.

22. *Ibid.*, p. 64.

23. In answer to Merleau-Ponty's argument in *Les aventures de la dialectique*, Sartre proposes a new use of the term "idéologue." "Ideology" had been used to name the philosophy of Destutt de Tracy (*Éléments d'idéologie*), Pierre Cabanis and others who continued the work of Condillac in France. The "idéologues" were interested in tracing the genesis of ideas understood in the Lockean sense. The second meaning was Marx' usage to indicate the underlying philosophical viewpoint expressed in a pattern of culture (*Die deutsche Ideologie*). Sartre has introduced a new meaning by labeling "ideologists" all those non-original philosophers who are dedicated to the task of developing the seminal concepts of dominant philosophies and philosophers. He names three periods of philosophy dominated respectively by Descartes and Locke, Kant and Hegel, and, finally, Karl Marx. Cf. *Critique*, p. 17.

In *Matérialisme et révolution*, "matter" had been declared the chief obstacle to a rational conception of a revolutionary philosophy. Quite obviously, since in its monistic materialism leaves no room for a consistent account of human freedom. The reformulation of the concept in Sartre's latest philosophy entails the same metaphysical dualism we have noted above. Every consciousness has its object; every *praxis* has its field of the "practico-inert." The practical terms "work," "project," "need," are the intentional correlatives for others taken from the practico-inert: "tool," "end" ("counter-end"), "interest" (or "destiny" or "counter-destiny"), and the like. Each individual *praxis* is conceived as a "totalization," or organization of means and ends in the surrounding inertial field; and each individual organization of this field implicates others in one way or another (competition or cooperation). Social relations are thus one resultant of the balance of forces achieved in the manipulation of matter. Given that man's individual need is felt under conditions of scarcity in the means to fulfill that need, social strife is a further natural concomitant of the manipulation of matter.

The element of determinism enters the picture, at the most rudimentary level, in the form of a practical exigency:

There is . . . a dialectical movement and a dialectical relationship within the *praxis* between action as a negation of matter (both with regard to its present organization and its future reorganization), and matter as a real and docile support of the current reorganization, which is the negation of the action. And that negation of the action—not to be mistaken for its failure—can only come about [reading "se produire" for "se traduire," which is inept] within the action in terms of action itself; that is, its positive results, insofar as they are inscribed in an object, turn against the original action, and within it, as objective and negative exigencies.[24]

24. *Ibid.*, p. 230.

(E.g., clearing of forest for planting produces a status of *defor-estation*, which in turn creates a further need to overcome the problem of soil erosion.)

In the further reaches of the dialectic, when the multiplicity of the individual *praxeis* have achieved their materialized result, serialization of the separate subjects in the practico-inert field, there arises an "anti-dialectic" of the original constitutive dialectics, which are organized anew into a created "social space": when the "dialectic of nature" is transformed into the domain of the "practico-inert," man's original freedom begins to feel the pinch of necessity, and is ordered according to a foreign principle. This new order is lived under the conditions of scarcity (of means to fulfill ends), and only a new invention may bring about further development. That invention is assembly (*rassemblement*) according to a common social goal, a new "totalization" of the original multiple activities; e.g., a collection of serialized individuals becoming a group. The action of the group is to refuse the necessity of the anti-dialectic, in whose field it is impossible to live due to the conditions of scarcity and the resultant competition.

In other words, the original dialectic exemplifies man's liberty, which is expressed in the free projection of individual goals. But since many subjects are projecting conflicting goals, there results a serial ordering of individual projects due to the scarcity of the means for realizing these goals. If freedom is expressed in the original dialectic (*dialectique-nature*), necessity finds its expression in the anti-dialectic, the negation of the original dialectics, considered as external to each other and plural in number. Sartre uses the term "anti-dialectic" to indicate that the free human activity of the original dialectics finds its negation in the domain of the practico-inert, where the "passivization" and alienation of the subject are determined by the subject's identification with the tools of his work and the objects they produce. The contradictions that arise from the conflicting goal-seeking activities are likewise necessary; but they create conditions under which it is impossible to live. A new invention, the creation of a peculiarly human domain, is necessary to contravene the original necessity. Ultimately, then, human freedom is a social phenomenon, and is experienced as the (practical) necessity of surpassing the initial necessity which restricts human freedoms in the realm of the practico-inert. In terms of social organization, the first dialectic (*dialectique-nature*) constitutes a *physis*, but produces an "*antiphysis*" and an "anti-humanity," which in its turn produces its *antiphysis* in the human domain of "the free relations between men," expressed in a new dialectic which Sartre calls "*dialectique-culture*." The locus of this domain, and the object of *dialectique-culture*, is the totalization of the human world in the historical enterprise.[25]

If the exposition of the historical process in this short compass seems absurdly complicated, it should be pointed out that Sartre himself is not unaware of the density of his thought; he states, in describing the second (anti-dialectic) stage of a "constituted" dialectic,

> Thus, just as the dialectic surpasses the material conditions [of its operation] by conserving them in its very negation, so materiality considered as an implacable necessity of the practico-inert surpasses the free *praxis* of each person, i.e., the multiple current dialectics, in order to conserve them within itself as the indispensable means of making its own *weighty* machinery turn.[26]

The third stage of the constituted dialectic is the minimal societal construct upon which any further "constituting" dia-

---

25. The preceding is a paraphrase of Sartre's conclusion to the first book of the *Critique*, entitled "De la *praxis* individuelle au pratico-inerte," pp. 375-377.
26. *Ibid.*, p. 376.

lectics must be based. New contradictions will produce new inventions, and new serializations will produce new assemblages; and so history, according to the later Sartre, will be lived, if not written.

The remainder of Sartre's first volume of the *Critique* is designed to examine the "rationality" of the concepts of social science: "class," "social struggle," "right," "duty," "institution," and "state."

In summary, I have been attempting to show that Sartre's philosophical career represents a direct line of development from his early rejection of French academic idealism through three graduated phases: in the phenomenological period, his influences are primarily Husserlian and Heideggerian; in the transitional and polemical period, he was defending his earlier philosophy against "misinterpretations"; and in the final stage, that of the present day, he has moved toward a studied revision of orthodox Marxist doctrine.

Throughout, he has never lost sight of his original intuition, that man cannot be defined in terms of an essence and that to be understood man must be considered in terms of his own free activity. There is no inherent contradiction between the philosophy of the individual expressed in *L'Être et le néant* and that of human history considered as the development of human institutions, expressed in *Critique de la raison dialectique.* One might even say that *L'Être*, as a phenomenological study of "human reality," was calculated to lay down the ontological conditions for having a psychological experience of any kind at all, while the *Critique* seeks to explain the conditions making possible a specifically social experience. Both are "eidetic" studies, both show a tremendous debt to Hegel's logic, but neither controverts whatever might be found to be true in a first-order scientific study, be it in psychology, social psychology and sociology, or history itself. Anyone who reads the entire Sartrean philosophical corpus will come away from it with an impression that Sartre is anything but a "simple, guileless fool." [27] He is not without guile, nor overwhelming by virtue of his simplicity.

27. *See* Herbert Luethy, "The Void of Jean-Paul Sartre," *The Anchor Review, No. 2* (Garden City, 1957), pp. 251-254.

BIBLIOGRAPHY OF THE PRINCIPAL PHILOSOPHICAL WRITINGS OF
JEAN-PAUL SARTRE

I: 1. *L'Imagination.* 3rd printing, Paris, 1950. Original edition:
Paris, 1936.
—Translation by Forrest Williams, *Imagination,* Ann Arbor,
1962.
    1.1 "Structure intentionnelle de l'image," *Revue de Méta-
physique et de Morale,* 45 (1938), 543-609.
    1.2 "Une idée fondamentale de la 'Phénoménologie' de
Husserl, l'intentionnalité," *Nouvelle Revue Française,*
52 (1939), 129-132.
  2. *L'Imaginaire: Psychologie phénoménologique de l'imagina-
tion,* 18th printing, Paris, 1948. Original edition: Paris, 1940.
—Anonymous translation, *Psychology of Imagination,* New
York, 1948.
    2.1 *Esquisse d'une théorie des émotions.* 2nd printing,
Paris, 1948. Original edition: Paris, 1939.
—Translation by Bernard Frechtman, *The Emotions:
Outline of a Theory,* New York, 1948.
  3. *L'Être et le néant: Essai d'ontologie phénoménologique,*
Paris, 1943.
—Translation by Hazel Barnes, *Being and Nothing-
ness: An Essay on Phenomenological Ontology,* New
York, 1956.
    3.1 "La transcendance de l'Ego," *Recherches Philoso-
phiques,* 6 (1936), 85-123.
—Translation by Forrest Williams and Robert Kirk-
patrick, *The Transcendence of the Ego: An Existen-
tialist Theory of Consciousness,* New York, 1957.
    3.2 *Réflexions sur la question juive,* Paris, 1946.
—Translation by George J. Baker, *Anti-Semite and
Jew,* New York, 1948. Another translation by Mary
Guggenheim in *Partisan Review* (Spring 1946), and
also as "Portrait of the Anti-Semite," in *Existentialism
from Dostoevsky to Sartre,* ed. W. Kaufmann, New
York, 1956.
    3.3 *Baudelaire,* Paris, 1947.
—Translation by Martin Turnell, *Baudelaire,* Norfolk,

Connecticut, 1950.

3.4 *Saint Genêt, comédien et martyr*, Paris, 1951.
—Translation by Bernard Frechtman, *Saint Genêt: Actor and Martyr*, New York, 1964.

II: 4. "Matérialisme et révolution," *Les Temps Modernes*, 1 [1] (1946), 1537-1563; 1 [2] (1946), 1-32.

5. "Qu'est-ce que la littérature?" *Les Temps Modernes*, 2 [1] (1947), 769-805, 961-988, 1194-1218; 2 [2] (1947), 77-114. Included in *Situations*, vol. 2, Paris, 1948.
—Translation by Bernard Frechtman, *What is Literature?* New York, 1949.

6. "Les communistes et la paix," *Les Temps Modernes*, 8 [1] (1952), 1-50, 695-763; 9 [2] (1954), 1731-1819.

6.1 "Réponse à Lefort," *Les Temps Modernes*, 8 [2] (1953), 1571-1629.

6.2 "Opération 'Kanapa,'" *Les Temps Modernes*, 9 [2] (1954), 1723-1728.

III: 7. "Questions de méthode," *Les Temps Modernes*, 13 [2] (1957), 338-417, 658-697.
—Translation by Hazel Barnes, *Search for a Method*, New York, 1963.

8. *Critique de la raison dialectique: précédé de Question de méthode*, Vol. 1, Paris, 1960.

GEORGE L. KLINE
Leszek Kołakowski and the Revision of Marxism[*]

I. *Introduction*

In 1906, seventy-five years after Hegel's death, Benedetto Croce published a vigorous critical study under the title *What is Living and What is Dead in the Philosophy of Hegel*.[1] The seventy-fifth anniversary of Marx's death came and went in 1958. Now, six years later, it is perhaps time for a similarly

---

[*] An earlier, and much shorter, version of this essay was read at the Thirteenth International Congress of Philosophy in Mexico City (September 1963). It is included in the *Proceedings* of the Congress (Mexico City, 1965) under the title "Philosophic Revisions of Marxism." Some of the material on the early Russian revisionists (Secs. IV and V) has appeared in German in my article, "Theoretische Ethik im russischen Frühmarxismus," *Forschungen zur osteuropäischen Geschichte* (West Berlin), 9 (1963), 269-279.

1. Benedetto Croce, *Ciò che è vivo e ciò che è morto della filosofia di Hegel: Studio critico seguito da un saggio di bibliografia hegeliana*, Bari, 1906.

comprehensive philosophical study of Marxism. The present essay might even be construed as, in part, a preliminary exploration along these lines. On the question of what is *vivo* and what *morto* in Marxist philosophy, I shall make my own position clear from the outset: What is dead, or at least dying, is an orthodoxy based principally on the writings of Engels and Lenin; what is alive, or at least viable, is that form of "revisionism" inspired partly by the early writings of Marx himself and partly by other, especially Kantian and existentialist, modes of thought.

In social-psychological terms: it is revisionism which attracts the more sensitive and intelligent among contemporary Marxist-Leninists; orthodoxy satisfies the less sensitive and intelligent, or the intellectually conformist and politically ambitious.

This is quite understandable. Compared to the deadness of philosophical orthodoxy, revisionism in general—and Marxist revisionism in particular—is vital and exciting. Nothing is duller than the writings of epigoni, however impressive the thought of the masters whose doctrines they repeat. Orthodox Platonists, Aristotelians, Thomists, Cartesians, Spinozists, Kantians, Hegelians, Marxists, Leninists, Deweyans, Whiteheadians, Husserlians, and Wittgensteinians are dreary creatures. But not everyone can be an innovator; hence the importance of revisionism. For it occupies the viable middle ground between two intellectual extremes: the unrealizable extreme of absolute doctrinal innovation [2] and the realizable but deadening extreme of absolute doctrinal reiteration.[3] So long as philosophical and

2. Cf. the recent statement by an American philosopher: ". . . philosophers do not invent, and a wholly original philosophy, if one could be formulated, would be beyond our understanding." (Robert E. Gahringer, "Analytic Propositions and Philosophical Truths," *Journal of Philosophy*, 60 [1963], 495.)

3. *Eclecticism*—the mechanical combining of two or more doctrines— might be defined as "plural orthodoxy" or "poly-orthodoxy." The combining of incompatible doctrines produces *syncretism*. Since revisionists often modify received doctrines in such a way as to assimilate them to distinct and even opposed positions, the borderlines between

political doctrines are corrigible, they will be subject to revision—in the double sense of *review* and *reform*, of critical scrutiny and theoretical modification.[4]

The *term* "revisionist" has been used in English for at least a century in a technical legal sense, and since the 1870's in the special sense of a scholar who contributed to the "revision" of the "authorized" (King James) version of the Bible. The first widespread use of the term in its contemporary political and philosophical sense came with the attack upon the position of Eduard Bernstein (1850-1932) in the 1890's. German and Russian Marxists, with their predilection for abstract words ending in "ism" (e.g., "pauperism," "economism," "opportunism," "deviationism"), quickly branded Bernstein's views as "revisionism." The name has remained, primarily as a polemical term employed by the critics of revisionist writers.

But the fact and the idea of revisionism in philosophy and politics have very ancient roots. Indeed, the history of Western philosophy may be seen as a series of cumulative revisions, beginning with the Platonic revision of Parmenides and ending with contemporary revisions of Husserl, Heidegger, and Wittgenstein.[5] Of the major philosophers perhaps only Plato and

---

4. The double sense is suggested, if not made explicit, by the etymology of the term. In Latin *revidere* means: to look over, to inspect closely with a view to correcting or improving.

5. In between there would be, for example, the Aristotelian, Plotinian, and Augustinian revisions of Plato; the Lucretian revision of Democritus-*cum*-Epicurus; the Scholastic revisions of Aristotle; the Cartesian revision of the Scholastics; the Leibnizian, Malebranchean, and Spinozistic revisions of Descartes; the Berkeleyan and Humean revisions of Locke; the Fichtean and Schellingian revisions of Kant; the Schopenhauerian revision of Plato-*cum*-Kant; the Nietzschean revision of Schopenhauer-*cum*-Hegel; the Marxian, Roycean, Solovyovian, and Deweyan revisions of Hegel; and the Whiteheadian revision of Leibniz-*cum*-Hegel.

---

revisionism, eclecticism, and syncretism are not always sharp or clear. We shall see examples of their blurring in the case of the early Russian "Kantian" and "Nietzschean" Marxists, and, to a degree, in Kołakowski himself.

Hegel and, with qualifications Kant and Peirce, are original enough to be considered not only "unorthodox" but also "non-revisionist."

Revision is thus a natural and productive aspect of intellectual life. Yet Leninists and Stalinists have made "revisionism" a term of abuse, denying that Marxism-Leninism can ever be justly or usefully revised, and branding every attempted revision as heresy and betrayal—a product of political reaction or counterrevolution. This strategem is not new. The first wave of German and Russian revisionism, which threatened to dilute the purity of orthodox Marxism in the decade after Engels' death (1895), was stoutly resisted in Germany by Karl Kautsky (1854-1938) and in Russia by G. V. Plekhanov (1856-1918), L. I. Akselrod,[6] Lenin, and others. The second, and more restricted, wave of revisionism which, in the 1920's, splashed against the rigid breakwaters of Leninist orthodoxy was violently beaten off by the ideological spokesmen of Soviet Leninism. The third and largest wave of revisionism, released by Stalin's death in 1953, has been resisted with unprecedented violence—and on an unprecedented scale—by Communist authorities in Eastern Europe and China as well as the Soviet Union.

Revisionism is repeatedly linked to "bourgeois ideology." It is described as "the most dangerous manifestation of bourgeois ideology within the working-class movement." Revisionists are called agents of imperialism and reaction.[7] Index cards

6. Not to be confused with the Menshevik leader P. B. Akselrod. Lyubov Isaakovna Akselrod (1868-1946), a prominent woman philosopher among early Russian Marxists, wrote under the *nom de plume* "Ortodoks" ("The Orthodox") and is frequently referred to by the hyphenated name "Akselrod-Ortodoks."

7. For one example among many see G. S. Vasetski's introduction to *Protiv sovremennovo revizionizma* (Against Contemporary Revisionism), ed. by Vasetski and A. P. Butenko (Moscow, 1958), pp. 5, 6. This is a volume of translated essays by French Communist, Bulgarian, Chinese, East German, Hungarian, Polish, and Rumanian critics of revisionism. A recent example of official Soviet criticism of philosophical revisionism

in Soviet libraries refer readers from the heading "Revisionism, Philosophical," to the heading "Bourgeois Reaction, Philosophy of, and Revisionism"! There is, of course, a grain of historical truth in this polemical juxtaposition. Orthodox Marxist-Leninists regard Kantianism, Nietzscheanism, existentialism, and positivism as "philosophies of bourgeois reaction." And, as we shall see, each of these philosophies has in fact influenced one or another of the contemporary philosophical revisions of Marxism.

A recent Chinese Communist critic goes so far as to lump together "modern revisionism," "imperialist reaction," and "natural catastrophes," [8] thus suggesting that revisionism is a kind of "ideological catastrophe"—which from the official Marxist-Leninist viewpoint it may very well be.

The fury of the official onslaught upon Marxist revisionism sometimes seems designed to mask lingering doubts in high places about the purity of what passes for orthodox doctrine. The official "Marxist-Leninist" position is in fact often quite as heterodox as that of the declared, or even self-confessed, revisionists. But when doctrine or policy [9] is modified by

8. As reported in the New York *Times*.

9. There is, of course, a difference between modification of *doctrine* and modification of *policy*. Doctrinal tenets are either true or false, adequate or inadequate. Policies or plans of action, in contrast, are either realizable or unrealizable, "realistic" or "utopian." Present plans of action will be realized, or fail of realization, in the future. They are thus more like theoretical predictions of future developments than like theoretical generalizations about past or present states of affairs. However, this distinction is not central to my concern in the present essay. (See the related discussion of political and philosophical revisionism in Sec. II below.)

is the review of Henri Lefèbvre's *La Somme et le reste* (Paris, 1958), by the veteran polemicist B. E. Bykhovski, published in *Voprosy filosofii*, No. 7 (1964), pp. 112-122. Bykhovski calls Lefèbvre an "anarchizing petit-bourgeois blunderer" (p. 122) and a "hypocritical petit-bourgeois" who, with "extreme cynicism, acknowledges his own inner rottenness." Lefèbvre's book is a disgusting "ideological strip-tease" which leaves the author "in all his ideological-political nakedness" (p. 112). According to Bykhovski, Lefèbvre's "entire work serves as an ideological weapon of anti-Communist *partiinost*" (p. 122).

political leaders, the result is never referred to as a "revision," but rather as the "creative development of Marxism-Leninism." "Revisionism" in the narrow and pejorative sense in which the term is used by official critics turns out to be a name applied by the politically powerful to modifications of doctrine or policy introduced by the politically powerless, in directions which the former regard as a threat to "ideological purity" and political stability.

This characterization applies, of course, to the relationship between political leaders and intellectuals *within* a given Communist country or bloc; and it relates primarily to *philosophical* revisionism. In the case of *political* revisionism, and of relations *between* Communist countries and even blocs, the situation takes on added complexity. Both before 1929 and after 1948 (the dates which roughly demarcate the period of Stalin's absolute ideological authority in the international Communist movement) there have been, and continue to be, cases in which one Communist-bloc leader accuses another of revisionism. Before 1929 Bukharin, Zinoviev, Trotsky, and Stalin exchanged such charges—mostly in terms of left and right-wing "deviation." After 1948 Stalin and Tito exchanged similar charges. Since 1961 the Albanians have been calling Tito a revisionist; in 1964 the Chinese joined them in openly branding not only Tito but also Khrushchev as a "modern revisionist." There is, of course, more than a grain of truth in the charge—if Lenin be taken as the standard of orthodoxy on such questions as violent (revolutionary) versus nonviolent (evolutionary) "paths to socialism," or the question of "peaceful coexistence of states with different social systems." On such doctrinal issues Mao and Hoxha are demonstrably closer to Lenin than either Khrushchev or Tito. (They are also more reckless and irresponsible as political leaders; but that is another story.)

Many other examples of specific doctrinal revisions might be mentioned: Lenin's voluntarism and stress on the revolutionary role of the peasantry were widely regarded, before October 1917, as revisions of Marxism, but were universally hailed during the Soviet period as "creative developments of Marxism." Stalin, in the 1920's, proclaiming the revisionist political doctrine and program of "building socialism in one country," and repudiating Marxist-Leninist egalitarianism, branded his relatively orthodox opponents—Trotsky in the first case, Zinoviev in the second—as "anti-Marxists" and "enemies of Marxism." Khrushchev's Party Program of 1961 implicitly repudiated the doctrine and program of the "withering away" of the family which had been accepted by Marx, Engels, and virtually all of the "old Bolshevik intellectuals," but rejected by Stalin in 1936. The Program stresses the proposition that a new kind of family, the "firm, stable socialist family," has made its appearance on the stage of history, and is here to stay.

To these examples of *political* revisionism, we may add one or two instances of *philosophical* revisionism "from above." Stalin (in the late 1930's) quietly eliminated the dialectical law of the "negation of the negation," placing an un-Leninist emphasis upon "gradual" or "progressive" development (*postepennoye razvitiye*) in nature and history. Under Khrushchev (in the late 1950's), the suppressed law was cautiously reintroduced. Again, Stalin's *Marxism and Questions of Linguistics* (1950) introduced a series of unilateral revisions into Marxist-Leninist theory, including a sudden increase in respect for formal logic and a general de-emphasis of "dialectical logic." This particular revision has largely been preserved and even expanded (with respect to mathematical logic) under Khrushchev and his successors.

II. *Political and Philosophical Revisionism*

I have already introduced a distinction between political (or programmatic) and philosophical (or theoretical) revisions of Marxism. It is now time to define political revisionism in detail sufficient to permit us to distinguish it clearly from philosophical revisionism. (The remainder of this paper will constitute a definition, both implicit and explicit, of philosophical revisionism.)

Political revisionists—who are sometimes referred to by their critics as "deviationists"—reinterpret *facts* and revise *theories* concerning the history and status of "capitalism" and "socialism," modifying their socio-economic and political *programs* accordingly.[10] Political revisionists may be classified as either "moderate" or "extreme."

"Moderate" political revisionists accept the *fact* that mid-twentieth-century "capitalism," at least in Great Britain and the United States, is significantly "socialized"—in the sense of "planned, equitable, and cooperative"; and that Soviet-style "socialism" is to a considerable degree "capitalistic"—in Marx's sense of "competitive, exploitative, and non-egalitarian." From this *fact* they derive a revisionist *program*: stress on class collaboration rather than class struggle, economic and political cooperation with "capitalist" countries (this applies especially

10. Kołakowski notes, for example, that the factual question of whether workers are subject to absolute "pauperization" under capitalism (as Marx claimed and Bernstein denied) is of crucial importance to the policy of the international working-class movement. (Cf. his "Intelektualiści i ruch kommunistyczny" ["The Intellectuals and the Communist Movement"], *Nowe Drogi*, No. 9 (1956), pp. 22-31; German translation in L. Kołakowski, *Der Mensch ohne Alternative: Von der Möglichkeit und Unmöglichkeit, Marxist zu Sein* [Munich, 1960], p. 43. Hereafter this volume will be cited as *Mensch*.)

to Yugoslavia and Poland), and the peaceful transformation of capitalism into socialism.

All of this, as Soviet critics have been quick to point out, echoes the 1899 position of Eduard Bernstein, as well as that of European Social Democrats and British Laborites since the turn of the century.

Soviet critics who attack the revisionist doctrine and program of peaceful transformation or growth [11] of capitalism into socialism are forced to make a delicate distinction between this "counterrevolutionary, reactionary theory" [12] and the strikingly similar view put forward by Khrushchev at the Twentieth Congress of the Communist Party of the Soviet Union in February 1956. Khrushchev agrees with the revisionists—versus the Chinese and Albanian "dogmatists"—that the transition can and should be non-violent. But where the revisionists—according to Soviet critics—count on a "spontaneous" (*stikhiiny*), unplanned, and unguided process, Khrushchev sees a "deliberate" (*soznatelny*), planned, and guided one. However, to a dispassionate observer, the revisionists do not appear to rely as heavily on historical "spontaneity" or "drift" as their critics charge. Their disagreement with Khrushchev—and it is a real one—concerns the character and quality of the admitted planning or guidance. Khrushchev insists that all planning be centered in a single monolithic party; the revisionists are prepared to share decision-making and responsibility with other social and political groups.

The "extreme" revisionists go one step further, denying that any political party holds a monopoly on political skill, judgment, or dedication to the public interest. Questioning the principle of one-party rule, such revisionists welcome loyal opposition parties, socialist (but non-Communist) or agrarian

11. The Russian term *pererastaniye* means literally "growing over"; it might be rendered in Latinized English as "transcrescence."

12. Vasetski, *op. cit.*, p. 10.

in nature. Of course, the very idea of *loyal* political opposition is the sheerest heresy to an orthodox Marxist-Leninist.

Moderate political revisionism has been codified in the 1958 Program of the League of Yugoslav Communists, a document which Soviet critics stigmatize as the "catechism of contemporary revisionism." [13] Extreme political revisionism found some support in Poland in 1956 and 1957; but its most articulate spokesman has been the Yugoslav Milovan Djilas, whose views proved sufficiently offensive to the moderate revisionist leadership of the League of Yugoslav Communists to cost him several years in prison. Perhaps extreme political revisionism, by its very nature, is too subversive of established authority to be acceptable by any group or party. Philosophical revisionism lacks organized support or encouragement for rather different reasons. It remains the creation of isolated and lonely individuals scattered across Eastern Europe, of a few members (now mostly ex-members) of Western European Communist Parties, and of a very few of the less conspicuous among younger Soviet philosophers.

III. *Marxism as Ideology and as Philosophy*

This is not the place for a detailed discussion of the term or the concept "ideology" or of the relationship which ideology bears to philosophy and to the special sciences. However, we may note that the peculiar sense which Lenin gave to "ideology"—a sense still mandatory for Soviet Marxist-Leninists—makes it equivalent to "theory." In Lenin's view, all knowledge, whether true or false, adequate or inadequate, and all theory, whether rational or "rationalizing," is ideological. This means that all knowledge is a super-structural reflection of relations within the socio-economic base, hence, in a "class

---

13. *Loc. cit.* The phrase has been repeated *ad nauseam* by Soviet critics.

society," necessarily partisan to the interests of a given class. (This is Lenin's famous notion of *partiinost*.) Pushed to its logical extreme, the Leninist reduction of theory to ideology undercuts any distinction between ideology and science, or between ideology and philosophy. It is the root of a notorious Leninist aporia, which issues in the abortive attempt to carve out some place for genuine (in effect, though not in terminology, "non-ideological" or "supra-ideological") knowledge by interpreting "objective and absolute truth" as a product of the accumulation of partial and relative truths.

Marx's own notion of ideology was much more restrictive. In his characteristic—although by no means wholly consistent —view, ideologies are false theories (or, in his Hegelian terminology, forms of "false consciousness") of a special kind, namely, those which serve to mask or to "rationalize" the harsh realities of a given socio-economic system.

In the present discussion, "ideology" is used in a sense broader than Marx's but narrower than Lenin's. An ideology is understood to be a more or less coherent set of theoretical claims and practical (i.e., social and moral) value judgments which function to organize the commitment and action of social groups. It may serve this function equally well whether the theoretical claims involved are true, false, or indeterminate in truth-value. A philosophy, in contrast, is a coherent set of practical valuations and of theoretical claims of utmost generality, which, to be acceptable, must pass the internal test of self-consistency and the external tests of applicability and adequacy.[14] The special sciences (physics, chemistry, biology, etc.) are sets of theoretical claims of more limited generality and (ideally) free of value judgments. Both philosophy and the special sciences—unlike ideology—make essential truth-claims

14. For a masterly discussion of such criteria as relevant to "speculative philosophy" see A. N. Whitehead, *Process and Reality* (New York, 1929), Pt. I, ch. i.

and stand or fall with the success or failure of these claims.[15]

Philosophies, like the special sciences, are essentially corrigible, hence inherently subject to revision. Philosophers and scientists are "revisionists" both by temperament and by training. But ideologists permit only the kind of pseudo-revisions "from above" which we have already discussed.

Contemporary ("third wave") revisionists of Marxism are more self-conscious and reflective about the nature of, and the need for, philosophical revision than were their "first wave" predecessors around the turn of the century. Leszek Kołakowski (b. 1927) is probably the leading theorist of philosophical revisionism, as well as the most productive philosophical revisionist, of his generation. He points out that not only Marxism but also phenomenology and psychoanalysis, as movements, include an orthodox group "which can do nothing but repeat the original formulae without variation," as well as a more creative and independent revisionist group. Kołakowski considers Bergson's philosophy, in contrast, to be a position which has not advanced beyond its first formulations; today it has (orthodox) "admirers" but no (revisionist) "offspring" or "continuers." [16]

He goes on to say that the "humanist left," for which he considers himself—and is widely considered—a spokesman, is marked by an attitude of "revisionism" in the sense of "perma-

15. Readers familiar with the pragmatist theory of truth (e.g., Dewey's) will recognize that this method of distinguishing philosophy from ideology would be closed to a consistent epistemological pragmatist. For the pragmatist, practice provides the only means of validating truth-claims, whether in ideology or philosophy, or indeed science. The distinction which I am using presupposes an epistemological realism rather than a pragmatism. But this is not the place to defend such a presupposition.

16. L. Kołakowski, "Kapłan i błazen" ("The Priest and the Jester"), *Twórczość*, No. 10 (1959); *Mensch*, p. 276. In Pawel Mayewski's English translation (in Marie Kuncewicz, ed., *The Modern Polish Mind* [Boston, 1962]) the passage in question occurs on p. 323.

nent criticism." [17] According to Kołakowski, to claim that any doctrine or method is exempt from revision is to abandon "science" in favor of "theology." [18]

Kołakowski puts the distinction between Marxism as ideology and as philosophy as that between "institutional" and "intellectual" Marxism.[19]

Institutional Marxism, in his view, is a set of doctrines and value judgments the content of which is fixed, and on occasion modified, by political authorities. Institutional Marxists do not have to be intellectually convinced of the truth, or even understand the meaning, of the doctrines which they profess. Thus, every institutional Marxist, Kołakowski wrote in 1957,

"knew" in 1950 that Lysenko's theory of inheritance was correct, that Hegel's philosophy was an "aristocratic reaction to the French Revolution," [20] that Dostoevski was a

17. L. Kołakowski, "Aktualne i nieaktualne pojęcie marksizmu" ("Up-to-date and Out-of-date Conceptions of Marxism"), *Nowa Kultura*, 8, 4/357 (1957), pp. 2, 7; *Mensch*, p. 22. Cf. also *Mensch*, pp. 29, 154.

18. It should be pointed out that the Polish term *nauka* (like the Latin *scientia*, Russian *nauka*, and German *Wissenschaft*) has a broad sense equivalent in English to "systematic intellectual discipline." In most European languages, but not in English, it makes good sense to describe history and philosophy as "sciences."

Kołakowski's identification of the *forma mentis* of what he calls "institutional Marxism" with dogmatic theology and "ecclesiasticism"—as opposed to reason and "science"—echoes Bogdanov's earlier indictment of Leninism as authoritarian and "theological." The focus of Bogdanov's criticism is Lenin's rambling and abusive attack on the Machian revisionists of Marxism—including Bogdanov himself—published in 1909 under the title *Materialism and Empiriocriticism*. (Cf. A. A. Bogdanov, "Vera i nauka" ("Faith and Science") in *Padeniye velikovo fetishizma* (The Fall of the Great Fetishism), Moscow, 1910.)

19. The term "institutional Marxism" had been used earlier by the Polish sociologist Stanisław Ossowski, but in a rather different sense.

20. The characterization of Hegel's philosophy as an "aristocratic reaction to the French Revolution" is Stalin's. (For details, see my article, "Some Recent Reinterpretations of Hegel's Philosophy," *The Monist*, 48 [1964], esp. pp. 36-37.) Kołakowski sometimes refers to institutional Marxism as "spiritual" or "intellectual" Stalinism. For understandable

"rotten decadent" and Babayevski an outstanding writer . . . , and that the theory of resonance in chemistry was obsolete nonsense. Every [institutional] Marxist knew this even though he had never heard of chromosomes, did not know what century Hegel lived in, had never read a word of Dostoevski, or worked his way through a secondary-school chemistry text.[21]

Of course, by 1956 institutional Marxists "knew" the contrary of most of these claims—and with equal assurance! Similarly, every institutional Marxist in the Soviet bloc was convinced before February 1956 that socialism could be achieved only through violent revolution—and after February 1956 that the only correct course was a "peaceful transition" from capitalism to socialism. Institutional Marxist scholars reversed themselves even more abruptly on the question of Marr's theories of language following Stalin's statements on linguistics in June 1950.[22]

In contrast, intellectual Marxism—for Kołakowski—is not a set of doctrines, but an attitude, a method, and a set of analytical categories. The attitude is rational, critical, and unsentimental; the method is historical and "deterministic," probing the causal interdependence of social phenomena, and stressing group antagonisms; the categories include "class," "ideology," "consciousness," "relations of production," etc. None of these categories is either crystal-clear or diamond-hard, although institutional Marxists insist that *all* Marxist categories are both.

The conception of "orthodoxy" or "doctrinal purity"—as Kołakowski points out—applies only to institutional or ideological Marxism. But such "purity" masks essential vagueness and ambiguity, required if ideological formulas are to remain fixed

21. Kołakowski, "Aktualne . . .": *Mensch*, p. 9.
22. *Ibid.*, pp. 7ff.

___

reasons, he has very little to say about Leninism. When he feels called upon to reject or revise a Leninist doctrine, he usually identifies it simply as "the current view." (Cf. *Mensch*, pp. 25, 132, 136.)

while their content changes.[23] Ideology, in Kołakowski's view, can never be eliminated; its social function—organizing the values of social groups, reinforcing belief and commitment for historical action—is vital.[24] But it can be "de-totalized"; its predatory and "imperialistic" grip upon intellectual life can be loosened and perhaps eventually broken.[25]

IV. *Philosophical Revisions of Marxism: A Historical Sketch*

In terms of the distinction outlined above, "revisionism" may be defined as the label which ideological or institutional Marxists apply to unauthorized changes in the content of philosophical or intellectual Marxism—to the extent that these changes call into question the "purity" of Marxist ideology.

Revisionism was possible in the decade after Engels' death because Marxism had not yet become a required ideology, sanctioned by political power; to use Kołakowski's term, it

23. Cf. *ibid.*, p. 35.

24. Kołakowski's use of the term "ideology" is plainly closer to Marx's than it is to Lenin's. In the loose Leninist sense of the two terms, "ideology" can be described as "scientific." But, in Kołakowski's view, it is only the "satraps of ideology with scientific pretensions" who boast of their country's "scientific foreign policy, scientifically guided painting and music, [and] scientifically grounded patriotism." (*Mensch*, pp. 25f, 36.) In such passages Kołakowski appears to be using both terms in a narrow sense, as do those French revisionists who reject the idea of a "scientific ideology" as a contradiction in terms. (See, for example, Henri Lefèbvre, *op. cit.* [fn. 7], p. 741.) In this they follow Eduard Bernstein who, a half-century earlier, had emphatically denied that Marxism, socialism, communism, or any other "ism" could be scientific. (*Wie ist wissenschaftlicher Sozialismus möglich?*, Berlin, 1901, p. 35.)

25. Such a loosening of the grip of authoritarian and coercive ideology is involved in what Bogdanov had described as the "fall of the great fetishism" in his book of that title (see fn. 18 above). Kołakowski sometimes refers to the "institutionalization" of Marxism as a "fetishizing" process. (Cf. "Intelektualiści . . .": *Mensch*, p. 56.)

had not yet been "institutionalized." [26] Following upon the "institutionalization" of Marxism-Leninism in the Soviet Union in the late 1920's, revisionism was effectively excluded from Soviet intellectual life. Its appearances since then, even during the cultural "thaw" of 1956, have been feeble, sporadic, and quickly suppressed. Outside the Soviet Union, however, revisionism was still possible within the Communist parties of Eastern and Western Europe; it flowered briefly after Lenin's death in 1924. The third, and greatest flowering, of course, came in the "socialist" countries of Eastern Europe, especially Yugoslavia and Poland, in the decade after Stalin's death.[27] This was possible because the rigidity of institutional Marxism was temporarily relaxed, most fully in 1956-1957.

Philosophical revisions of Marxism, both early and late, have been concentrated in the areas of epistemology and ethics, which are the least-developed portions of classical Marxist theory. Marx himself wrote almost nothing on theory of knowledge; Engels' "theory of reflection"—which Marx allegedly endorsed—has always seemed to most non-Marxists, and to many thoughtful Marxists, both primitive and inadequate.

As for ethics, Marxism, like Hegelianism, is oriented toward the social and "world-historical" and away from the individual and ethical. Hegel wrote no treatise on ethics; indeed—as Kierkegaard pointed out long ago—there is no room in the Hegelian system for an autonomous ethic. The same is true of Marxism, in the sense that it admits no intrinsic or irreducible ethical criteria. In his maturity, Marx, following late Hegel, held, in effect, that whatever is the objective outcome

26. In both the ordinary and the Kołakowskian senses of the term, i.e., both embodied in socio-political institutions and hardened into a required ideology, modifiable only "from above."

27. In Yugoslavia, political revisionism may be traced back to Tito's break with the Cominform in 1948, but *philosophical* revisionism would appear to be a phenomenon of the post-Stalin period, as it was elsewhere in Eastern Europe.

of the immanent dialectic of history is right. Lenin—the "Machiavelli of revolution"—added that whatever serves the cause of revolution and the building of socialism is right. From these two criteria, *historical* and *strategic,* respectively, there is no possibility of appeal to any independent *ethical* criterion. Marxist revisionists in ethics have been concerned—either explicitly or implicitly—to discover or devise precisely such a criterion.

The elements of Marxism which were rejected by revisionists, both early and late, are more closely associated with the work of *Engels* than with that of Marx. This applies not only to the epistemological "theory of reflection," already mentioned, but also to ontological materialism and the generalization of the laws of the Hegelian dialectic from human history to the whole of nature. These three doctrines, taken over by Lenin, form the core of orthodox dialectical materialism. A fourth Engels-Lenin tenet, not emphasized by Marx, is the claim that the history of philosophy from the pre-Socratics to the present day can and should be interpreted as a struggle between two "camps"—that of the "pure" philosophical materialists and that of the "pure" philosophical idealists. Of course, Leninists admit that some major philosophers have been relatively "impure" waverers. But where less partisan historians see complexity and subtlety, Leninists apply their exclusive and exhaustive "either-or" (materialism *or* idealism, and *tertium non datur*). Thus Plato, Hume, and Dewey are "idealists"; Aristotle, Locke, and Spinoza are "materialists." Kołakowski wrote a large book on Spinoza partly to show that the seventeenth-century thinker must be considered "neither-nor." [28] Similarly, half a century earlier, the Russian Machians (Bog-

28. See L. Kołakowski, *Jednostka i nieskończoność: Wolność i antynomie wolności w filosofii Spinozy* (The Individual and the Infinite: Freedom and the Antinomy of Freedom in Spinoza's Philosophy) (Warsaw, 1958).

danov, Lunacharski, et al.) had insisted that their own "empiriocriticism" was a "neither-nor" position. The chief philosophical aim of Lenin's *Materialism and Empiriocriticism* (1909) was to reduce the "third" positivistic position of the Russian Machians to a form of idealism. In the end, Lenin argued, there is no essential difference between Mach or Avenarius and Bishop Berkeley! [29]

The revisionists who reject these four Engels-Lenin tenets, however, are virtually unanimous in accepting what they take to be *Marx's* central contributions: his philosophy of history, his theory of social change, and his general critique of capitalism and religion. Some of them appeal to the "young Marx" of the Paris Manuscripts of 1844 for support in their rejection of Engels and Lenin.

Nietzsche once said that there are only a handful of possible philosophical systems—which accounts for the similarity of the great traditions of Indian, Greek, and German thought. Be that as it may, there does seem to be no more than a handful of possible revisionist positions. At least, the pattern of contemporary Marxist revisionism bears a striking resemblance to that of the first wave of Russian revisionism, in which revisions in ethics took three forms, paralleled by three forms of revision in theory of knowledge:

ETHICS	EPISTEMOLOGY
1. Kantian	1. Kantian
2. Nietzschean	2. positivist (Machian or "empiriocritical")
3. "Spinozist"	3. "quasi-Kantian" (Plekhanov's theory of hieroglyphs)

In both ethics and epistemology, group No. 1 was most hetero-

29. Lefèbvre, in his revisionist writings, claims to have moved beyond both materialist and idealist "postulates" in ontology. (Cf. *op. cit.* [fn. 7], p. 754.)

dox, group No. 3 most nearly orthodox; group No. 2 stood between the other two, although somewhat closer to the first than to the third. The members of the first group were: P. B. Struve (1870-1944), S. N. Bulgakov (1871-1944), and N. A. Berdyaev (1874-1948); of the second group: A. A. Bogdanov (real name Malinovski: 1873-1928), V. A. Bazarov (real name Rudnev: 1874-1939), A. V. Lunacharski (1875-1933), and S. Volski (real name Sokolev: 1880-1936?); of the third group: Plekhanov, Akselrod-Ortodoks, and Alexandra Kollontai (1872-1952).

I shall say comparatively little about the epistemological revision of the post-Engels, post-Lenin, or post-Stalin period, and this for two reasons: (a) Contemporary revisionists have written very little on epistemology, and (b) the epistemological views of the earlier revisionists were for the most part slavishly derivative from Western sources—from Kant and Cohen or from Mach and Avenarius. It is curious that Lenin, who devoted an entire book to criticism of the Machians, paid not the least attention to the Kantian and Nietzschean revisions in ethics, which were not only philosophically more significant, but also represented a more serious threat to the "doctrinal purity" of Marxist-Leninist ideology.

Although a serious Kantian revision developed within the German Marxist movement in the 1890's, the German Marxists felt *no* intellectual sympathy for, or ideological interest in, the philosophy of Nietzsche. Even the Kantian revision in Germany—as seen in the writings of its founder, Eduard Bernstein—was primarily political and only peripherally philosophical. Bernstein's "Kantianism" amounted to the claim that the advent of socialism should not be regarded as the necessary outcome of an immanent historical dialectic, but as the possible (and eminently desirable) realization of a freely chosen ideal. Similarly, Bernstein defined exploitation (in 1901) in ethical, rather than economic terms, as "the morally reprehensible utilization" of one man by another or others.[30] But his opposition of *Sollen* and *Sein* was vague and programmatic, not analytical or systematic.

There appear to have been at least two reasons for the exceptional interest in Kant and Nietzsche on the part of early Russian Marxists: (a) the historical circumstance that by the middle of the last decade of the nineteenth century Kant and Nietzsche had become the two commanding figures in Western-European philosophy, displacing the Hegelianism and the anti-Hegelian positivism that had prevailed until then; (b) the doctrinal attractiveness of Kant's *ethical* criterion and Nietzsche's *aesthetic* or *cultural* criterion as supplements to, or substitutes for, the *historical* criterion (for evaluating human acts and institutions) offered by Hegel and Marx.

The Kantian Marxists attempted to defend the autonomous individual against the historical "heteronomy"[31] of classical Marxism by providing a theoretical *justification* of "proletarian morality." They placed positive emphasis on the dignity and responsibility of the individual moral agent. The Nietzschean Marxists undertook to free the creative individual from the restricting confines of normative ethics by a *repudiation* of every kind of "ought." On this point Nietzsche and Marx concurred: both the proletariat as a class and the *Übermensch* may be said to stand "beyond (bourgeois-Christian) good and evil." The Nietzscheans placed positive emphasis on the freedom and spontaneity of the individual artistic creator. It is probably no accident that several of the Nietzschean Marxists were productive writers and literary critics, or that Maxim Gorky was for a time closely associated with this group.

30. Bernstein, *op. cit.* [fn. 24], p. 12.
31. What I here call "historical heteronomy" or the "heteronomy of history" is very close to what Kołakowski calls "ethical Hegelianism" or "pseudo-Hegelianism"—i.e., the reduction of ethical to historical criteria and the corollary assumption that whatever is historically necessary is *ipso facto* morally justified. (See Sec. V below.)

Kant's ethics includes at least four distinct, and partially independent, strands: (1) its "formalist" stress on the *a priori* nature of moral judgment; (2) its "normative" emphasis upon duty and the right; (3) its "individualist" insistence that the human person must always be treated as an end-in-himself and never as a means only; [32] (4) its "libertarian" claim that men's actions, although "phenomenally" determined, are "noumenally" free. It was the third point—ethical individualism—which was accepted by all of the Russian Kantian Marxists, but especially by Berdyaev, who disliked Kantian "formalism" and "normativism," the points in which Kant is most sharply opposed to Nietzsche. Thus, while emphasizing the dignity and autonomy of the individual, Berdyaev rejected "abstract obligation" in favor of ethical creativity and passion. Indeed, it might be more accurate to describe Berdyaev at the turn of the century as a "Nietzschean-Kantian" Marxist. Such a position goes beyond revisionism, bordering on eclecticism, if not syncretism. It is not surprising that within a decade Berdyaev had largely abandoned Kant in favor of Nietzsche and was beginning to develop his own form of religious existentialism.

The theoretical difficulties which faced the Russian Kantian Marxists—as exemplified by Berdyaev—cluster around the related notions of *progress, freedom,* and *individuality:*

(1) Berdyaev's "postulate" of an objective ethical *progress*

---

32. Kant himself maintains that this dictum—"Act so that you treat humanity, whether in your own person or in that of another, always as an end and never as a means only"—is deducible from, or even equivalent to, the first formulation of the categorical imperative, namely: "Act only according to that maxim by which you can at the same time will that it should become a universal law." In fact, this is the case only if supplementary assumptions concerning human rationality and the relation of being rational to being an end-in-oneself are (at least tacitly) introduced. (The quotations from Kant are from *Foundations of the Metaphysics of Morals,* tr. by L. W. Beck [Indianapolis, 1959], pp. 47, 39.)

in the historical (hence phenomenal) realm,[33] coupled with a denial of the noumenal as "other-worldly," is open to the criticism which Kant himself leveled at "uncritical" or "pre-critical" philosophies, namely, that the *empirical* evidence which would establish the reality of such progress is not, and in principle cannot be, conclusive.

(2) The Kantian stress on individual moral *freedom* and responsibility proved incompatible with the Hegelian-Marxian stress on the determined collectivity of the "world-historical." Sensing this, Berdyaev moved from historical determinism to a "semi-positivist" mitigation of determinism and ultimately to an assertion of the central existential reality of human freedom.

(3) Kant's dictum that the *individual person* must be treated as an end, never as a means only, is left in the Kantian-Marxist formulation without serious philosophical support. Berdyaev's non-Kantian comrades could justifiably claim that, from a Marxist point of view, such a principle remained theoretically ungrounded and in no way binding upon revolutionary practice.

The Nietzschean Marxists were unanimous in welcoming Nietzsche's repudiation of the ethics of duty and his celebration of the ethics of volition and creativity. But they disagreed sharply on the question of whether volition and creativity should take individual or collective forms. The more individualistic, and thus more orthodoxly Nietzschean, among them were Volski and Lunacharski; the more collectivistic, hence

33. More generally, Berdyaev denies that the moral order is confined to an unknowable "noumenal" realm, as Kant had held. Rather, he insists, it is to be found in the "uniquely real phenomenal world [sic], in the *progress* which is taking place in the cosmic and historical process and realizing the 'realm of ends.'" (N. A. Berdyaev, *Subektivizm i individualizm v obshchestvennoi filosofii* [Subjectivism and Individualism in Social Philosophy] [St. Petersburg, 1901], p. 75.) The first English translation of selections from this important Kantian-Marxist document is scheduled to appear in 1965 in *Russian Philosophy*, ed. by James M. Edie, James P. Scanlan, and Mary-Barbara Zeldin, with the collaboration of George L. Kline (Chicago, 1965).

more orthodoxly Marxist, Bogdanov and Bazarov. However, the "collectivism" of the last-named—as opposed to the normative collectivism of later Leninists and Stalinists—was meant to be voluntary and non-normative. The Nietzschean collectivists maintained that under socialism individuals would freely desire to subordinate their interests to those of the social whole. The Leninists and Stalinists declared that individuals were duty-bound to do so.

Ranged on a spectrum from most to least individualistic, the Nietzschean Marxists would stand: Volski, Lunacharski, Bogdanov, Bazarov. Their views cannot be examined further here;[34] instead I offer three brief summary comments on the Nietzschean revision of Marxism in Russia:

(1) Nietzsche is closer to Marx than is Kant. Kant's approach to individual morality is "pre-Hegelian" and non-historical, Nietzsche's is "post-Hegelian"—theoretically as well as chronologically—and "culture-historical." To be sure, Nietzsche regards the "dead" weight of past history as an obstacle to present creativity. But for him this creativity is not an end in itself; rather it serves *future* history, enriching the cumulative culture which is in process of becoming.

(2) The theoretical tension between the ethical positions of Marx and Nietzsche reaches its peak in the question of egalitarian versus élitist ethics. Who is to shape and reshape cultural values? According to Nietzsche, the solitary few; according to Marx, the solidary many. The Nietzschean Marxists tried to have it both ways. Their disagreement on the matter of individual versus collective creativity was symptomatic of the deeper difficulty attendant upon any attempt at

34. For further details see my article, "Changing Attitudes toward the Individual" in C. E. Black, ed., *The Transformation of Russian Society* (Cambridge, 1960), esp. pp. 618-623; also my "Theoretische Ethik im russischen Frühmarxismus," *Forschungen zur osteuropäischen Geschichte*, 9 (1963), esp. pp. 275-279.

a synthesis of the ethics of Nietzsche and Marx. Once again, revisionism merges into eclecticism, coming dangerously close to syncretism.

(3) The Nietzschean Marxists followed Nietzsche in rejecting traditional theism while accepting a "new" immanentistic and humanistic religion. Gorky and Lunacharski declared that "God-building" (*bogostroitelstvo*) should be the "religion of the proletariat," whose god would be mankind itself as the collective creator of historical culture. Such a view is more compatible with Nietzsche's position than with Marx's; it was impatiently repudiated by Lenin and his followers.

The "revisions" which cropped up here and there in the Communist parties of Eastern and Western Europe during the 1920's were too meager and sporadic to permit ready classification. There seem to have been brief flirtations with Nietzschean Marxism among the Czechs. A form of positivism (officially labeled "mechanism") flourished in Moscow and Leningrad until it was "liquidated" by Soviet authorities in 1930. The most serious philosophic contributions were those of Georg Lukács,[35] then living in Vienna, and of Ernst Bloch (both born in 1885).

The "neo-Hegelianism" of Lukács' *Geschichte und Klassenbewusstsein* (1923) was promptly attacked by the Soviet guardians of Marxist-Leninist orthodoxy. Lukács himself was not slow in repudiating the "revisionist tendencies" of his own work. After the Second World War, and his return to Buda-

35. Although a Hungarian by birth, Lukács has written and published all of his philosophical works in German, a language in which he is thoroughly, if somewhat ponderously, at home. An informed and thoughtful study of Lukács is Morris Watnick, "Relativism and Class Consciousness: Georg Lukács," in L. Labedz, ed., *Revisionism: Essays on the History of Marxist Ideas* (London and New York, 1962), pp. 142-165. The same volume contains a rather less satisfactory treatment of Bloch by Jürgen Rühle: "The Philosopher of Hope: Ernst Bloch," pp. 166-178.

pest, following a long stay in Moscow,[36] he heaped abuse upon Western "neo-Hegelians" such as Maurice Merleau-Ponty (1908-1961) who persisted in regarding *Geschichte und Klassenbewusstsein* as Lukács' major contribution to Marxist theory. In essays written in 1946-47 and published in 1951 under the title *Existentialismus oder Marxismus* Lukács sharply attacked the kind of Kantian-existentialist ethics later to be defended by Kołakowski (see below, Sec. V). His attack is focused upon Sartre, Simone de Beauvoir, and Merleau-Ponty.

Bloch, in a series of works which began to appear in 1918 and continued into the 1950's, offended Marxist-Leninists by distinguishing a "warm stream" and a "cold stream" in Marxist thought—the former characterized as the impulse to freedom and revolutionary action, the latter as the impulse to realistic and deterministic analysis of social situations. In opting for the former, Bloch undercut Marxist determinism, stressing the openness of the historical process and the efficacy of human hope. In 1954 he listed Plato, Aristotle, Leibniz, Kant and Hegel —idealists all—among the intellectual forerunners of his own "principle of hope," [37] conspicuously omitting the materialists from whom Marxist-Leninists are expected to trace their philosophical lineage. Such heresies have long given Bloch a place apart among both revisionists and anti-revisionists in the Soviet bloc. It is not surprising that within a month of the erection of the Berlin wall in August 1961 he should have sought political asylum in Western Germany—becoming the only

36. One of Lukács' most important philosophical contributions is his study of Hegel's early works (through the *Phenomenology* of 1807), published as *Der junge Hegel: Über die Beziehungen von Dialektik und Ökonomie* (Zürich and Vienna, 1948). In a private conversation (Budapest, September 1960) Lukács admitted that, if he had remained in the Soviet Union after the Second World War, this book—although it had been substantially completed *before* the war—would probably never have been published.

37. Bloch's *magnum opus*, which runs to 1,657 closely printed pages, is called *Das Prinzip Hoffnung*, 2 vols. (Frankfurt-am-Main, 1959).

major Marxist philosopher to do so. He is now (1964) a professor of philosophy at the University of Tübingen.

The third wave of Marxist revisionism, touched off by Khrushchev's denunciation of Stalin (and, more guardedly, of "Stalin*ism*") at the Twentieth Party Congress in February 1956, was much more massive and potentially destructive of orthodoxy than either of its predecessors. In many ways it presents a magnified image of the first wave of German and Russian revisionism: the Kantian and Nietzschean revisions in ethics have been replaced by a single "Kantian-existentialist" or "anthropological" revision (whose most articulate spokesman is Kołakowski). Corresponding to the early and relatively orthodox "Spinozistic" revision in ethics is a relatively orthodox "Hegelian" revision. In epistemology the early Kantians and Machians have been succeeded by neo-positivist or "analytical" Marxists. This is not strange in view of the historical continuity in theory of knowledge which runs from Kant through Avenarius and Mach to the Vienna Circle and beyond.

The forms of contemporary philosophical revisionism may be represented schematically as follows:

ETHICS	EPISTEMOLOGY
1. Kantian-existentialist	1. ————
2. ————	2. neo-positivist or "analytical"
3. "Hegelian"	3. ————

Spaces left blank indicate lack of interest or failure to develop clear positions. This applies to the "Kantian-existentialists" and "Hegelians" with respect to epistemology; to the "positivists" with respect to ethics.[38]

38. Some of the Czech and Polish positivists appear to favor an "emotivist" or "noncognitivist" *metaethics* in the style of A. J. Ayer and C. L. Stevenson, although they have not, so far as I know, worked it out in any detail. Henryk Skolimowski's Oxford dissertation, *Polish Analytical Philosophy* (including a discussion of what he calls "analytical-linguistic Marxism"), is scheduled for publication by Oxford University Press.

As in first-wave revisionism, group No. 1 is most heterodox, No. 3 most nearly orthodox. A majority of contemporary revisionists began as Leninist-Stalinists, shifting intellectual position rapidly between 1954 and 1957, in the wake of such political and ideological traumas as Khrushchev's de-Stalinization drive (February 1956), and the Polish and Hungarian "Octobers" (October-November 1956). Russian revisionists of the first wave had passed through a similarly rapid intellectual evolution during the late 1890's and early 1900's; but all of them had *begun* as revisionists, if moderate ones. They were confronted with no ideological or "institutional" Marxism from which to break away.

Contemporary "Kantian-existentialist" revisionists make very few explicit references either to Kant or to existentialist thinkers. However, their *critics* have been quick to note, and deplore, the "marriage of Kantianism and existentialism" entailed by their ethical position—as an official Polish critic expressed it in 1958.[39] Many of them seek a ground for ethical individualism in "der junge Marx," especially the eloquent if not always coherent critique of "alienation" and "reification" of the Paris Manuscripts of 1844. In fact, some revisionists use "early Marx" not only against Engels and Lenin but also against "late Marx." The early Kantian and Nietzschean Marxists might have done the same, except that the Paris Manuscripts were not published until 1932.

The neo-positivists as a group are in retreat from speculative philosophy, whether Hegelian or Marxist-Leninist; they express their contempt for "fuzzy dialectical thinking" by calling it "Hegelianism" (Russian *gegelyanstvo*). They include some of the younger logicians and philosophers of science, in the Soviet Union as well as Poland and Czechoslovakia, who are professionally concerned with questions of mathematical logic, axiom-

39. Adam Schaff, *Spór o zagadnienia moralności* (The Dispute about Moral Principles) (Warsaw, 1958), p. 67.

atization, information theory, cybernetics, and even computer-programming. Some of the relevant names are L. Tondl (Czechoslovakia), Helena Eilstein (Poland), and A. A. Zinoviev (Soviet Union). The last named is the author of an interesting monograph on *Philosophical Problems of Many-Valued Logic*, published in English translation in 1963.

The "Hegelians" have also withdrawn from speculative philosophy—into history and commentary. They have been active in translating and commenting upon Hegel's *Phenomenology* and certain other works, and in tracing the influence of Hegel upon Marx. This group includes Tadeusz Kroński (Poland), who died young in 1958; Milan Sobotka and Ivan Dubský (Czechoslovakia); Lukács (Hungary); and, to a lesser extent, E. V. Ilyenkov (Soviet Union).

Philosophically, the Kantian-existentialists may be said to be oriented toward the individual human *future*, the Hegelians toward the collective "culture-historical" *past*, and the positivists toward *neither*. The latter are non-temporally oriented—as befits thinkers whose noetic models are to be found in mathematics and formal logic.

V. *The Individual, the Collective, and the March of World History*

The remainder of this essay will be devoted to an analysis of the Kantian-existentialist attempt to reconcile individual moral responsibility with the objective march of world history. I shall try to bring out the parallel between the position developed around the turn of the century by one of the most sensitive and intelligent of young Russian Marxists of that period, Nicholas Berdyaev, and the position elaborated in the late 1950's by one of the most sensitive and intelligent of young Polish Marxists of our own day, Leszek Kołakowski.

The first Kantian revision in ethics took its origin in the

efforts of several gifted and erudite young Marxists (notably Berdyaev and Struve) to answer the central question of Marxist ethics, namely: How can *one* of the competing class-moralities be *proven* objectively superior to the other(s)? What is the *justification* for the Marxist commitment to proletarian, rather than bourgeois or feudal-aristocratic, morality?

The classical Marxist answer to these questions, according to Berdyaev, takes two forms, one *logical*—not, of course, in the sense of formal logic but in the Hegelian sense of a "logic of history"—the other *psychological.* (It might be more precise to say that the Marxist answer appeals to two kinds of *criteria,* one historical, the other psychological.) The first states that proletarian morality *will* in fact triumph, as the necessary outcome of the "immanent conformity to law of the historical process." [40] The second states that because of its class-interests the proletariat as a class necessarily *desires* the triumph of this morality.

Berdyaev finds these answers true but inadequate. To establish that proletarian morality *will* triumph or that the proletariat *desires* its triumph is not to prove that it *deserves* to triumph. One might consistently—though falsely [41]—assume that history is realizing an *immoral* ideal, e.g., increasingly efficient exploitation. The march of history, Berdyaev admits, might be a moral retreat rather than an advance.

To speak of the historical realization of an *immoral* idea is, of course, to make at least implicit appeal to an independent ethical criterion reducible neither to "class psychology" nor to the "logic of history." Berdyaev himself makes this appeal explicit when he proposes a third answer, an "objectively *ethical*"

40. Berdyaev, *op. cit.* [fn. 33], p. 63.

41. Berdyaev's confidence in the falseness of this assumption (the "postulate of historical regress") is based on his confidence in the truth of his own counter-assumption (the "postulate of historical progress"). See above, pp. 133f.

grounding of proletarian morality, which is essentially Kantian. Proletarian morality, Berdyaev asserts, must be proven *worthy* to triumph by being shown to correspond more closely than any competing class-morality to the principle that individuality is an end in itself "giving moral sanction to all else and needing no sanction for itself." [42] (Any proffered psychological or historical sanction—Berdyaev seems to recognize—would entail a vicious circularity.) In asserting, with Kant, that the formal distinction between good and evil precedes all sense experience and hence all historical determinations, Berdyaev adopts a position which is not only un-Marxian but also un-Hegelian.

Kołakowski, in 1957, sharply qualifies Berdyaev's "postulate of historical progress," placing clearer emphasis upon the moral autonomy of the existing individual than Berdyaev was prepared to do in 1901. His ethical revision of Marxism, although independent of Berdyaev's,[43] is parallel to it in many ways and encounters many of the same theoretical difficulties.

Kołakowski stands at the turbulent confluence not only of Marxist and non-Marxist intellectual currents but also of the disparate streams of recent Polish positivism,[44] contemporary Anglo-American analysis, and Continental existentialism. His terminology and rhetoric reflect a hospitable cosmopolitanism which sometimes verges on the eclectic—a danger, as we have seen, in all revisionism. Thus, he stresses the "mutual exclusiveness" of values and loyalties and admits the "permanent possibility of tragedy." He sees an "incurable antinomy" in the realm of human values, an antinomy which no possible social

42. Berdyaev, *op. cit.*, p. 74. Berdyaev renders the Kantian term *Selbstzweck* by the closely parallel Russian term *samotsel*.

43. In answer to an inquiry, Kołakowski declared (letter to the author dated May 8, 1961) that he was not familiar with Berdyaev's early writings. In a recent conversation (Warsaw, December 1964), he stressed the lack of historical continuity between what I have called "first-wave" and "third-wave" revisionism.

44. Tadeusz Kotarbiński was one of Kołakowski's teachers of philosophy.

change could alleviate. He speaks of "anguish," "absurdity," "authenticity," "risk," "decision," "commitment." Yet in the same breath he can refer to "pseudo-questions," "many-valued logics," the distinction between "normative" and "descriptive" judgments, the need for empirical enquiry. Only occasionally does he use purely Marxist terminology, as in discussing the "contradiction" between the "façade" and the "content" of a social system. Compared to his fellow-Marxists in the Soviet Union and elsewhere in Eastern Europe, most of whom still speak in the accents of the nineteenth century, Kołakowski's idiom is modern indeed.

The ethics of Kierkegaard is close in many essential respects to that of Kant.[45] Kołakowski, an avowed atheist and anti-cleric, seems to have derived a great deal from both thinkers—although his public acknowledgments are to Sartre and (usually in a peripheral or illustrative way) to the nineteenth-century Russian thinkers Belinski and Herzen. Of the four strands in Kantian ethics,[46] Kołakowski seems most firmly committed (like Berdyaev) to ethical individualism but also (unlike Berdyaev) to normativism. He hedges on the question of freedom, attempting to combine an assertion of individual free choice with an acceptance of social determinism. He implicitly rejects Kant's formalism, insisting that "duty is only the voice [*głos*]

45. Both Kant and Kierkegaard stress duty, responsibility, the certainty of moral intentions (as opposed to the contingency of consequences), freedom, and the universality of moral relationships. Strangely enough, Kołakowski, who appears to accept all of these emphases, refers to Kierkegaard only once and in passing—as an example of an irrational defender of a "mystified" (Christian) ideology! ("Odpowiedzialność i historia": *Mensch*, p. 64.) The only existentialist to whom he refers both explicitly and affirmatively is Sartre. In one place he mentions Jaspers and Marcel as "Christian existentialists." ("Kapłan i błazen," *Twórczość*, No. 10 [1959], p. 67; "The Priest and the Jester," *The Modern Polish Mind*, p. 303. For some reason both names are omitted from the German translation; see *Mensch*, p. 252.)

46. See above, p. 133.

of a social need." [47] Thus for him morality is not *a priori* but, in Kantian terms, *a posteriori* and "heteronomous." That is, as a Marxist he sees the ground of moral obligation not in the individual moral agent but rather in a historically conditioned social structure ("stratum" or "class").

Yet Kołakowski's "Responsibility and History" [48] is an im-

---

47. "Odpowiedzialność . . .": *Mensch*, p. 126.

48. "Odpowiedzialność i historia," *Nowa Kultura* (Warsaw), September 1, 8, 15, and 22, 1957. A heavily abridged and occasionally inaccurate English version is included in *Bitter Harvest*, ed. by E. Stillman (New York, 1959), pp. 94-125. This translation appeared originally in four installments in the journal *East Europe* during 1957 and 1958. Selections from it, slightly revised, are included in Arthur P. Mendel, ed., *Essential Works of Marxism* (New York, 1961), pp. 347-370. A full and generally accurate German version (authorized translation by Wanda Bronska-Pampuch) is included in *Der Mensch ohne Alternative: Von der Möglichkeit und Unmöglichkeit, Marxist zu Sein* (Munich, 1960), pp. 57-141. A French translation by Anna Posner appeared in Sartre's journal *Les Temps Modernes*, 13 [2] (1958), 2049-2093; 14 [1] (1958), 264-297. In the present essay all page references will be to the German translation, indicated thus: *Mensch*, p. 120.

The puzzling German title, which Kołakowski informs me (letter of November 10, 1962) was supplied by the publisher, seems to mean something like: "The (Individual) Human Being, without Either-Or's (e.g., *either* Stalinist *or* reactionary)." The subtitle refers to the impossibility, for a self-respecting thinker, of being an *institutional* Marxist and the possibility of being an *intellectual* Marxist (see Sec. III above).

The German translation is lively and graceful; its departures from the Polish original—beyond a few fairly minor errors—appear to be of three kinds: (1) omission of material of primary interest to Polish readers, e.g., Tuwim's witty Polish quatrain about the symbiosis of city and country-side, which Kołakowski applies to the relationship between philosophy and the special sciences: the latter supply the former with food, receiving garbage from it in return (omitted: *Mensch*, p. 167); (2) deletion of certain politically-sensitive references, e.g., mention of the abortive proposals (ca. 1956) for establishing a non-official philosophy journal in the Soviet Union (omitted p. 55); (3) inclusion of a few politically-sensitive passages which did not figure in the published Polish version, e.g., the comment that, from the point of view of institutional Marxism, to doubt the official (Stalinist) interpretation of the Hitler-Stalin pact is to embrace fascism (p. 75).

passioned defense of individual moral autonomy against the heteronomy of history, or, as he puts it, an affirmation of the "total responsibility of the individual for his own deeds, and the amorality of the historical process." [49]

Like Belinski, whom he mentions here, and Herzen, whom he does not, Kołakowski condemns every sacrifice of the existing individual to an abstract historical future. "What right do I have," asks the Intellectual (interlocutor of the Revolutionary [50] in the brief dialogue with which "Responsibility and History" opens), "in the name of that speculative dialectic of the future to renounce at present the supreme values of human existence?" [51] And the Intellectual continues: It is immoral to sacrifice the present for the future; and to give up truth, self-respect, and moral values is to sacrifice the future itself.[52]

Kołakowski characterizes the Hegelian-Marxist philosophy of history as a "historiosophy," [53] using a nineteenth-century term still more or less current in Polish—and to some extent German and Italian—philosophical discourse, but strange to English and American usage. In a general way, Kołakowski's

---

49. "Odpowiedzialność . . .": *Mensch*, p. 123.
50. These are the terms used in the English translation; the Polish words are *klerk* and *rewolucjonist* or *anty-klerk*. The German uses *Schöngeist* or *Clerk* and *Revolutionär* or *Gegner des Clerk*. The French uses *belle âme* or *clerc* and *révolutionnaire* or *anti-clerc*.
51. "Odpowiedzialność . . .": *Mensch*, p. 61.
52. *Ibid.*, p. 66.
53. The literal meaning of the term, of course, is "wisdom of history." In Polish it is *historiozofia*, in Russian *istoriosofiya*, in Italian *storiosofia*, in German *Historiosophie*. Kołakowski's translators—except for Pawel Mayewski, in his version of "The Priest and the Jester," and the anonymous translator of the selections included and revised by Mendel in *Essential Works of Marxism*, both of whom use "historiosophy"—have rendered it as "philosophy of history," *philosophie de l'histoire*, and *Geschichtsphilosophie*. But this blurs the specificity of the term as well as its distinction from terms designating non-Hegelian-Marxist philosophies of history. One of the first systematic uses of the term was by the Polish Hegelian August Cieszkowski in *Prolegomena zur Historiosophie*, 1838.

use of the term "historiosophical" parallels Berdyaev's earlier use of "logical" (see above, p. 141), although it is pejorative, whereas Berdyaev's references to the "logic of history" were not. Historiosophy, which is an expression of the "cunning of the *Weltgeist*," is for Kołakowski a nightmare of abstractions.

In the world of historiosophy, he writes,

> there are no more individuals: they appear only as instances of [general] ideas, bearing the mark of their species upon their foreheads. In that world we do not eat bread and butter; we restore our labor power, which is consciously organized for the purposes of socialist construction. We do not sleep; we regenerate cerebral tissue for creative work in realizing the *Weltgeist*; we talk not to men but to carriers of ideas, which are themselves only representatives of certain conflicting social forces in the gigantic march of history . . . [Thus] we move from the swamp of everyday life to the madness of abstract life, as if we were passing from a brothel to a monastery.[54]

In Kołakowski's view, the historiosophical assurance that "we can read the future of the world as reliably as a railroad timetable" is an "insane illusion."[55] He derides the "poverty of prophetic historiosophy" and urges "historiosophers" to confine themselves to a study of the historical necessities of the *past*.[56]

But Kołakowski's principal objection to historiosophy is not so much theoretical as moral. It is not merely that we cannot be as sure of the future as we can of the past, but that "the greater the degree of certainty we have concerning the intentions of the demiurge [of history], the greater the threat" to our moral sanity, the greater the danger that we will substitute criteria of historical effectiveness for ethical criteria.[57]

In more theoretical and general terms, Kołakowski character-

54. "Odpowiedzialność . . .": *Mensch*, pp. 118-119.
55. *Ibid.*, p. 117.
56. *Ibid.*, pp. 105, 140.
57. *Ibid.*, pp. 115, 120.

izes the reduction of ethical to historical (or "historiosophical")
criteria as "ethical Hegelianism" or "pseudo-Hegelianism." [58]
Its extreme form is *Stalinism,* a position which entails the
claim that whatever serves socio-economic "progress" is morally
obligatory, thus erasing the distinction between the "historically
progressive" and the "morally right." [59] But since it is difficult,
if not impossible, to know just which present acts or policies
will contribute to future historical progress, Stalinists (or
"institutional Marxists") permit others to make this decision
for them.[60]

Kołakowski sharply rejects the value-dogmatism (he calls it

58. The late Tadeusz Kroński, referred to above (p. 140) as a leading
Polish "Hegelian" revisionist, undertook—without mentioning Kołakowski
by name—to refute Kołakowski's implied indictment of Hegel. Kroński
insists that "Hegel was very far from that historiosophical immoralism
which, in its theoretical reflections, willingly and light-heartedly sacrifices
millions of human beings to a 'higher good' . . . ," adding that it is a
mistake to identify Hegel as (among other things) "an immoralist who
sacrifices morality to a 'higher end'—namely, 'the welfare of the state'. . ."
("Hegel und die Probleme der Geschichtsphilosophie," *Studia filozoficzne,*
No. 1 [1962], pp. 100, 104. This special issue contains translations into
English, French, German, and Russian of articles originally published in
Polish in the same journal. Kroński's article had first appeared in No. 3
[1958], pp. 42-75. It was translated into German by Jan Garewicz and
Inga Ogonowska.)
59. Kołakowski comments ironically that if the "Demiurge of Historical
Progress" decides to speak in the voice of Genghis Khan [Stalin?], the
"historiosophers" will offer him their services. And if the zoologist pre-
dicts the coming of an "age of ants," historiosophers will advise people to
accept their fate quietly, leaving their human skeletons on the anthills of
the world. (*Mensch,* p. 92.)
60. "Odpowiedzialność . . .": *Mensch,* pp. 99, 138; cf. also pp. 90, 95f.
With clear, if implicit, reference to the Soviet Union under Stalin,
Kołakowski adds: "A whole social system has made of [historiosophy]
an instrument of moral masochism." (*Ibid.,* p. 105.) An instance of such
masochism is the tormented feeling on the part of Soviet citizens—a
feeling carefully cultivated by the Stalinist leadership—that in doubting
Yablochkov's priority over Edison in the invention of the electric light,
they were calling into question the principle of the dictatorship of the
proletariat! (*Ibid.,* p. 74.)

"axiological absolutism" [61]) of the "normative interpretation of historiosophy," i.e., the deduction of *Sollen* from *Sein* (an explicitly Kantian polarity), of duty from historical necessity. Such dogmatism is closely related to the judging of present acts in terms of their anticipated consequences for world history.[62]

Putting the point in theoretical terms (in a section of his essay entitled "Conscience and Social Progress") Kołakowski writes: "Practical choice in life is made in a world defined by *'Sollen'* and not by *'Sein.'* . . . It is not true that historiosophy determines our main choices in life. Our moral sensitivity [*poczucie*] does this." This sensitivity, he adds, must not be dulled or smothered by the "opiate of the *Weltgeist.*" [63] Putting the point in personal and political terms, he declares: "We are not Communists because we have recognized communism as a historical necessity; we are Communists because we have joined the side of the oppressed against the oppressors. . . ." [64]

Generalizing his tormented reflections on the "historical

61. The Polish phrase is *absolutyzm aksiologiczny*, correctly translated into German as *axiologischer Absolutismus* (*Mensch*, p. 61), but garbled in English into the meaningless "axiomatic absolutism." (*Bitter Harvest*, p. 95; *Essentials of Marxism*, p. 351.)

62. "Odpowiedzialność . . .": *Mensch*, pp. 61, 89f. Early in 1962 Kołakowski completed a two-act play called "Entrance and Exit," expressing his earlier critique of Stalinizing historiosophy in allegorical form. Political authority is symbolized by the dentist; the "people" are his patients who "enter and exit" from the waiting room. A pompous apologist for the dental (read: "political" or "ideological") profession declares: "I have reason to believe that the new dentist will be even better than the former one. Also the system he will use will be better. I reveal to you a deep truth that life has taught me—every dentist is better than the last one. This truth will help you go through life with faith in the sense and reason of everything, with faith in justice and progress." The play was closed down by Warsaw authorities after less than a week; its full text has never been published. (See the New York *Times*, January 21, 1962.)

63. *Mensch*, pp. 99, 124, 137.

64. *Ibid.*, p. 124.

crimes of Stalinism," Kołakowski asks—unconsciously echoing
Berdyaev: "If crime is the law of history, does knowledge of
this law justify one in becoming a criminal?" [65] His answer is
unequivocal:

> No one is absolved from the moral responsibility for support-
> ing a crime merely because he is convinced of its inevitable
> victory. No one is exempted from the moral duty to oppose
> a political system, a doctrine, or a social order which he
> considers to be base and inhuman on the ground that he
> also believes them to be historically necessary.[66]

Kołakowski in 1957 had experienced more of the "horrors of
world history" than Berdyaev in 1901 could imagine. And he
was painfully aware that many of the worst of them had been
perpetrated by professed Marxist-Leninists:

> Between obedience to history and obedience to the moral
> imperative yawns an abyss on whose brink the great historical
> tragedies have been played: the tragedies of conspiracies and
> insurrections doomed to disaster, and the opposed tragedies
> of collaboration with crime based on a belief in its inevitabil-
> ity. On both of these brinks the moral drama of the revolu-
> tionary movement in recent years has also been played out.[67]

To avoid vicious circularity, Kołakowski says, we must
acknowledge the logical priority of social progress *or* of moral
values, but not both. To define social progress in terms of
moral values violates the principles of historical materialism;
to accept any value as absolute violates the principles of the
dialectical method.[68] This strikes me as a succinct and accurate
formulation of the dilemma of Kantian Marxism.

As we have seen, Kołakowski wishes to remain a Marxist,

65. *Ibid.*, p. 61.
66. *Ibid.*, p. 89.
67. *Ibid.*, p. 102.
68. *Ibid.*, p. 97.

even at the risk of undermining his Kantian commitment to "moral values" and individual moral responsibility. As a Marxist he accepts one form of the doctrine of "historical inevitability" —a social determinism which reduces men's moral convictions to reflections of their social circumstances. He repeatedly insists that such determinism is compatible with individual moral responsibility.[69] But in at least one place he sensibly suggests that the determinism in question may be "statistical" rather than "strict."[70]

> The fate of an individual cannot be determined by the gener-alized laws of the class struggle, any more than the behavior of an individual particle of a gaseous substance [i.e., a gas molecule] can be predicted from the general laws governing the mechanics of gases [i.e., statistical mechanics], although the latter remain valid with respect to aggregates.[71]

There may be a very high probability, even a "statistical quasi-certainty,"[72] that at least one of the thousand people standing

69. In 1959 Kołakowski added that the contemporary problem of rec-onciling individual responsibility with historical determinism is essentially the same as that which Augustine debated with the Pelagians—namely, to what extent can an individual resist the forces external to him which influence his behavior? To what extent is he responsible for his own actions? ("Kapłan . . .": *Mensch*, p. 257; "The Priest and the Jester," p. 307.) The subtitle of this erudite essay is "Reflections on the Theo-logical Heritage in Contemporary Thought." Late in 1961 a young Polish intellectual told me that it was one of the most widely read and admired of Kołakowski's works.

70. This is a suggestion made in passing by Kant himself, but left undeveloped. See his "Idee zu einer allgemeinen Geschichte in Welt-bürgerlicher Absicht" (1784), in *Immanuel Kants Werke*, ed. by A. Buchenau and E. Cassirer, Berlin, 1922, 4, 151. Kant's own example is the statistical predictability of marriage, birth, and death rates—in sufficiently large populations—despite the element of free choice involved in such human actions.

71. "Istota i istnienie w pojęciu wolności" ("Essence and Existence in the Concept of Freedom") in *Światopoglad i życie codzienne* (World-View and Everyday Life) (Warsaw, 1957), p. 117.

72. "Odpowiedzialność . . .": *Mensch*, p. 122.

by a river bank will leap into the water to save a drowning child, but anyone who actually *does* so must have made his own (free) decision. And no one who fails to do so has any right to appeal to historical, social, or even biological necessity as an excuse for his inaction. In Kołakowski's words:

> Neither our own supposedly irresistible passions ("I was unable to resist the impulse"), nor anyone's command ("I was a soldier"), nor conformity to social custom ("Everyone did that"), nor the theoretically deduced law of the Great Demiurge [of history] ("I thought I was acting for the sake of progress")—can be regarded as justification.

None of these kinds of determination "relieves the individual of moral responsibility, because none of them eliminates the freedom of individual choice." [73]

In explicitly Kantian terms, Kołakowski asserts that certain human actions are ends-in-themselves, hence obligatory, and others are "counter-ends-in-themselves," hence absolutely forbidden. If moral values are subordinated to the realization of historical necessity, then nothing in contemporary life can be considered an end in itself, and moral values in the strict sense lose their validity.[74]

For Kołakowski the free individual faces not a historical but a personal or "existential" future. Men who permit their own moral choices to be "historiosophically" determined are like

> tourists who scratch their names on the walls of dead cities. Everyone can . . . interpret himself historically and discover

73. *Ibid.*, p. 123. Cf. Sartre: ". . . tout homme qui se réfugie derrière l'excuse de ses passions, tout homme qui invente un déterminisme est un homme de mauvaise foi." (*L'Existentialisme est un humanisme* [Paris, 1960; first ed. 1946], pp. 80-81.)

74. *Ibid.*, p. 100. Sartre had used the term "counter-end" as early as 1946, in his essay "Matérialisme et révolution," published in the first volume of *Les Temps Modernes*.

EUROPEAN PHILOSOPHY TODAY

the determinisms to which he was subject while he was becoming what he now is, that is, in his past. But he cannot do this with respect to the person he has not yet become. He cannot infer his own future from historiosophical predictions.[75]

In order to do this, says Kołakowski, one would have to treat oneself as wholly in the past, in other words, as dead.

Such a claim sounds not merely "existentialist," but specifically Kierkegaardian. It suggests that Kołakowski may tacitly recognize the inconsistency of his attempt to combine moral autonomy with socio-historical heteronomy. When he sums up his position as involving: (1) ethical individualism ("only individuals and their actions are subject to moral evaluation"), (2) social determinism ("moral judgments are socially conditioned"), and (3) the right to moral judgment of political decisions and institutions [76]—he gives the impression of being most deeply committed to the first and third of his "theses," and quite possibly—like Berdyaev half a century earlier—on the way to abandoning, or at least drastically modifying, the second of them as inconsistent with the other two. Whether

75. *Ibid.*, p. 141.
76. Kołakowski lists three additional "theses," which I take to be less central. They are: (4) "The humanistic interpretation of value": theoretical determinism does not entail the value judgment that individuals are not responsible for their acts; (5) "The historical interpretation of value": *Sollen* is a form of *Sein;* (6) "The denial of pseudo-realistic criticism of moralizing utopias" (mistranslated in *Mensch*, p. 127, as "Die Negierung der pseudorealistischen Utopien"). Theses (2) and (5) express the Marxist side of Kołakowski's thought; theses (1) and (3) express the Kantian-existentialist side. Thesis (4) is an attempt to reconcile the two. I do not find it entirely convincing. Kołakowski claims to be able to preserve the integrity of moral freedom and responsibility in the face of what we know, or postulate, about social determinism. But the *value* judgment that a man is responsible for his acts presupposes the *cognitive* claim that he is free to act otherwise than he in fact does. And this cognitive claim, I would argue, *is* contradicted by determinism. (I have slightly rearranged Kołakowski's theses; thus my numbering does not entirely correspond to his.)

or not this is the case, Kołakowski's attempt to combine individual moral autonomy with a form of socio-historical heteronomy—although it is marked by moral passion as well as intellectual vigor—comes dangerously close to syncretism.

VI. Conclusion

Soviet critics explain the striking renaissance of both political and philosophical revisionism in the 1950's as "a manifestation of bourgeois ideology in the working class." [77] They attempt to account for its influence in Poland, Yugoslavia, Czechoslovakia, and East Germany, and its lack of influence in the Soviet Union, in terms of the relative newness of "socialism" in the first three countries and its relative maturity and stability in the last. The same reasoning, however, would lead one to expect serious revisionist tendencies in Rumania, Bulgaria, and Albania, where—in the post-Stalin decade—there has in fact been no evidence whatever of revisionism, either political or philosophical. A more plausible explanation is the greater rigidity and tighter ideological monopoly of institutional Marxism in Rumania, Bulgaria, Albania, and the Soviet Union. Whatever revisionist currents exist in those countries have long since been forced beneath the official surface into the "cultural underground"—along with (to use Soviet examples) non-representational painting, religious and erotic poetry, novels like Pasternak's *Dr. Zhivago* and Abram Tertz's *The Trial Begins*, and plays like I. Ivanov's *Is There Life on Mars?*

Similarly, the more plausible explanation for the flourishing of revisionism in the freer milieu of Poland and Yugoslavia, and to a lesser extent and for a shorter time in Czechoslovakia and East Germany, would seem to be, as a Bulgarian critic

77. Cf. e.g., M. A. Stepenski, *Sovremenny revizionizm i yevo filosofiya* (Contemporary Revisionism and its Philosophy) (Kursk, 1959), p. 4.

admitted in 1957, that it is "a reaction to dogmatic Marxism." [78] To be sure, the same critic added the qualification, "in its *form*" (presumably as opposed to its *content*). This qualification was omitted by Lukács, who recently characterized revisionism as a "reaction to Stalinism," [79] but insisted that he himself was *not* a revisionist, and indeed that revisionism must be resisted—though with persuasion rather than force.[80]

It is difficult to predict the further development of philosophic revisionism among contemporary Marxists. The major revisionist writings date from 1956-1957; since 1958 very little of philosophical significance has been published by Eastern European Marxists.[81] This is probably due less to failing interest or slackened intellectual vitality than to the increasing pressure of institutional Marxism; and such pressure shows little sign of abating. As a Soviet spokesman put it in 1958: "Either we destroy revisionism, or revisionism will destroy us; there is no

78. V. Naidenov, "Revisionism and Dogmatism in the Contemporary Working-Class Movement," *Novo Vreme*, No. 3 (1957): cited from the Russian translation in Vazetski, ed., *Protiv sovremennovo revizionizma*, p. 50.

79. The recent polemical writings of the official critics of Polish and Yugoslav revisionism have a distinctly Stalinist ring. This is not surprising. In attacking the anti-Stalinism of the revisionists, they are driven into a posture of "anti-anti-Stalinism," which, by negation of the negation—whether Hegelian or Aristotelian—brings them very close to Stalinism.

80. In a private conversation (Budapest, September 1960). Lukács, of course, is regularly attacked by Soviet polemicists—along with Marković, Lefèbvre, Kołakowski, Bloch, et al.—as a "leader of contemporary revisionism." In fact, his heresy would appear to be more political than philosophical: he was Minister of Culture in the short-lived Nagy regime (1956), which Soviet critics consider "counterrevolutionary." As we have seen, Lukács himself has insistently repudiated the "Hegelian" revisionism of his own early works, especially *Geschichte und Klassenbewusstsein* (1923).

81. Among the few philosophically significant publications of the period 1959-1964 I would include one or two of Kołakowski's essays, Karel Kosík's *Dialektika konkrétního* (Dialectic of the Concrete) (Prague, 1963), and a scattering of works by Yugoslav Marxist philosophers.

third way." The official campaign to root out revisionism has been unparalleled in scope and violence; it is hardly surprising that this campaign should have succeeded in driving most of the revisionists underground.

A Soviet critic has described the "logic of the revisionists" as moving from "rejection of Stalin in the name of Lenin" to "rejection of Lenin in the name of Marx," and finally to "rejection of Marxism generally." [82] This particular sequence applies more directly to political than to philosophical revisionism. The parallel sequence in philosophy would be: rejection of Engels and Lenin in the name of Marx, rejection of late Marx in the name of early Marx (and of Kant and Sartre or Wittgenstein and Carnap), and, finally, rejection of Marxism generally.

No contemporary revisionist has publicly taken this last step. But it seems likely that philosophical revisionists like Kołakowski might, if given the opportunity, move further away from Marxism—as Berdyaev and the other Kantian Marxists did after 1903—in the direction of existentialism, neo-Kantianism, or perhaps some new man-centered philosophy of their own. Such a move would represent a doctrinal loss to intellectual Marxism, and an ideological blow to institutional Marxism. But it would be a distinct gain for philosophy.

A final question: Will Khrushchev's departure from the Soviet political scene be followed by a fourth wave of philosophical revisionism like those which followed the death of Engels in 1895 and of Stalin in 1953? Thus far the official "de-Khrushchevization" campaign has spared Khrushchev's ideological pronouncements—perhaps a tacit avowal of his lack of stature as a Marxist-Leninist. His retirement leaves no ideological vacuum comparable to that created by the de-Stalinization campaign of 1956—which suggests that there is

82. Stepenski, *op. cit.*, pp. 29f.

not likely to be a significant wave of post-Khrushchev revisionism. But only the future can substantiate, or invalidate, that suggestion.

BIBLIOGRAPHY OF THE PRINCIPAL WRITINGS OF
LESZEK KOŁAKOWSKI

"M. Cornforth: Nauka przeciw idealizmowi" (M. Cornforth: Science versus Idealism), *Myśl Współczesna*, 11 (1951), 304-311.

"Avicenna—lekarz dusz i ciał" (Avicenna—Healer of Bodies and Souls), *Myśl Filozoficzna*, No. 3 (1952), pp. 36-55.

"Filozofia nieinterwencji: Głos w dyskusji nad radykalnym konwencjonalizmen" (A Philosophy of Non-Intervention: Contribution to the Discussion of Radical Conventionalism), *Myśl Filozoficzna*, No. 2 (1953), pp. 335-373.

Szkice o filozofii katolickiej (Sketches of Catholic Philosophy), Warsaw, 1955. Contains the following chapters:

(1) "Od autora" (From the Author).

(2) "Neotomizm w walce z postępem nauk i prawami czlowieka" (Neo-Thomism in Conflict with the Progress of the Sciences and the Rights of Man): reprinted from *Nowe Drogi*, No. 1 (1953).

(3) "Kwestia robotnicza w doktrynie politycznej Watykanu" (The Labor Question in Vatican Political Doctrine): reprinted from *Nowe Drogi*, No. 6 (1954).

(4) "O tak zwanym realizmie tomistycznym" (On So-Called Thomist Realism): reprinted from *Myśl Filozoficzna*, No. 1 (1954).

(5) " 'Prawa osoby' przeciwko prawom czlowieka" ('The Rights of the Individual' versus the Rights of Man): reprinted from *Myśl Filozoficzna*, No. 1 (1955).

(6) "Nauka przed sądem Ciemnogrodu" (Science before the Court of Ciemnogrod): reprinted from *Myśl Filozoficzna*, No. 2 (1953), pp. 374-388.

(7) "Metodologia księdza Kłosaka: Felieton filozoficzny" Father Kłosak's Methodology: A Philosophical Feuilleton): reprinted from *Myśl Filozoficzna*, No. 1-2 (1955), pp. 315-322.

(8) "Igraszki z djabłem" (Playing the Devil's Game): reprinted from *Po Prostu*, No. 15 (1954).

"Marxismus und personalistischer Freiheitsbegriff," *Das Problem der Freiheit im Lichte des wissenschaftlichen Sozialismus*. Konferenz der Sektion Philosophie der Deutschen Akademie der

Wissenschaften zu Berlin, 1-10 März, 1956, *Protokoll,* [East] Berlin, 1956, pp. 153-168. (This volume was later withdrawn from circulation by the East German authorities.)

Wykłady o filozofii średniowiecznej (Essays on Medieval Philosophy), Warsaw, 1956.

"O łatwości rozstrzyzniecia problemu nominalizmu" (On the Easy Solution of the Problem of Nominalism), *Myśl Filozoficzna,* No. 5 (1956), pp. 150-155.

"Problematyka historii polskiej filozofii i mysli społecznej XV-XVII w." (Problems of the History of Polish Philosophy and Social Thought in the Fifteenth to Seventeenth Century), in the volume Z *dziejów polskiej myśli filozoficznej i społecznej* (Toward a History of Polish Philosophical and Social Thought), ed. L. Kołakowski, Warsaw, 1956, I, pp. 9-43.

"Intelektualiści i ruch kommunistyczny" (The Intellectuals and the Communist Movement), *Nowe Drogi,* No. 9 (1956), pp. 22-31. (German translation in *Der Mensch ohne Alternative,* pp. 40-56, *see below.*)

"Aktualne i nieaktualne pojęcie marksizmu" (Up-to-date and Out-of-date Conceptions of Marxism), *Nowa Kultura,* No. 1 (January 27, 1957), pp. 2, 7. German translation in *Der Mensch,* pp. 7-39. English translation: "Permanent and Transitory Aspects of Marxism" in P. Mayewski, ed., *The Broken Mirror: A Collection of Writings from Contemporary Poland,* New York, 1958, pp. 157-174.

"Aktualność sporu o powszechniki" (The Timeliness of the Dispute about Universals) in the volume *Światopoglądowe i metodologiczne problemy abstrakcji naukowej* (Problems of Scientific Abstraction from the Standpoint of World-View and Methodology), Warsaw, 1957, I, pp. 113-160: reprinted from *Myśl Filozoficzna,* No. 2 (1956) pp. 3-32.

Światopogląd i życie codzienne (World-View and Everyday Life), Warsaw, 1957. Contains the following chapters:

(1) "Od autora" (From the Author).

(2) "Z czego żyja filozofowie?" (What Do Philosophers Live By?): reprinted from *Przegląd Kulturalny,* Autumn, 1956. German translation in *Der Mensch,* pp. 163-180.

(3) "Światopogląd i edukacja" (World-View and Education).

(4) "Światopogląd i krytyka" (World-View and Criticism).

(5) "Wizjonerstwo i dogmatyzm" (Utopianism and Dogma-

tism): reprinted from *Przegląd Kulturalny*, Oct. 27-Nov. 12, 1955.

(6) "O słuszności zasady: cel uświęca srodki" (On the Validity of the Maxim: The End Sanctifies the Means). German translation in *Der Mensch*, pp. 225-237. French translation by Michel Pavelec in *Les Temps Modernes*, 12 [2] (1957), 1357-1370.

(7) "Istota i istnienie w pojęciu wolności" (Essence and Existence in the Concept of Freedom).

(8) "Platonizm, empiryzm i opinia publiczna" (Platonism, Empiricism, and Public Opinion): reprinted from *Przegląd Kulturalny*, Summer, 1956. German translation in *Der Mensch*, pp. 216-224.

(9) "Katolicyzm i humanizm" (Catholicism and Humanism).

(10) "Antysemici" (The Antisemites): reprinted from *Po Prostu*, Summer, 1956. German translation in *Der Mensch*, pp. 181-190.

(11) "Światopogląd i życie codzienne" (World-View and Everyday Life). German translation in *Der Mensch*, pp. 191-215.

"Odpowiedzialność i historia" (Responsibility and History), *Nowa Kultura*, September 1, 8, 15, and 22, 1957. German translation in *Der Mensch*, pp. 57-141; abridged English translation in *East Europe*, 5, No. 12 (1957), pp. 12-15; 6, No. 2 (1958), pp. 17-21; 6, No. 3 (1958), pp. 24-28; 6, No. 5 (1958), pp. 12-16; reprinted in *Bitter Harvest*, ed. E. Stillman, New York, 1959, pp. 94-125; selections in *Essential Works of Marxism*, ed. A. Mendel, New York, 1961, pp. 347-370; French translation by Anna Posner in *Les Temps Modernes*, 13 [2] (1958), 2049-2093 and 14 [1] (1958), 264-297; Russian translation in *Gorkaya zhatva* (Bitter Harvest), ed. E. Stillman, New York, 1961, pp. 374-419.

"Co to jest socialism?" (What Is Socialism?), written for *Po Prostu* in 1956, but not published except in English and Russian translation: in *Bitter Harvest*, pp. 47-50; and in *Gorkaya zhatva*, pp. 86-90.

"Sens ideowy pojęcia lewicy" (The Ideological Significance of the Concept 'Left'), *Po Prostu*, No. 8/423 (1957), pp. 1-2, 4. German translation in *Der Mensch*, pp. 142-162.

Jednostka i nieskończoność: Wolność i antynomie wolności w filosofii Spinozy (The Individual and the Infinite: Freedom and the Antinomy of Freedom in Spinoza's Philosophy), Warsaw, 1958.

"Pochwała niekonsekwencji" (In Praise of Inconsistency), *Twórczość*, No. 9 (1958), pp. 88-94.

160   EUROPEAN PHILOSOPHY TODAY

"Karol Marks i klasyczna definicja prawdy" (Karl Marx and the Classical Definition of Truth), *Studia Filozoficzne*, No. 2 (1959), pp. 43-67. Russian and English abstracts, pp. 68-69; abridged English translation in *Revisionism: Essays on the History of Marxist Ideas*, ed. L. Labedz, London and New York, 1962, pp. 179-187.

"Determinizm i odpowiedzialność" (Determinism and Responsibility) from the volume: *Fragmenty Filozoficzne: Seria druga* (Philosophical Fragments: Second Series) [A Festschrift for Tadeusz Kotarbiński], Warsaw, 1959, pp. 25-43.

"Mistyka i konflikt społeczny: O możliwości interpretacji mistycyzmu metodami materialistycznego pojmowania dziejów" (Mysticism and Social Conflict: On the Possibility of Interpreting Mysticism by the Methods of the Materialist Conception of History), *Studia Filozoficzne*, No. 3 (1959), pp. 3-51. (Russian and English abstracts, pp. 52-53.)

"Pierre Bayle: Critique de la métaphysique spinoziste de la substance," in the volume *Pierre Bayle, le philosophe de Rotterdam* (études et documents publiés sous la direction de Paul Dibon), Paris, 1959, pp. 66-80.

"Światopogląd XVII stulecia" (The Seventeenth-Century World-View) in the volume *Filozofia XVII wieku: Francja, Holandia, Niemcy* (Seventeenth-Century Philosophy: France, Holland, Germany), texts selected and annotated by L. Kołakowski, Warsaw, 1959.

"Kapłan i błazen" (The Priest and the Jester), *Twórczość*, No. 10 (1959), pp. 65-85. German translation in *Der Mensch*, pp. 250-280; English translation by Pawel Mayewski in Maria Kuncewicz, ed., *The Modern Polish Mind*, Boston, 1962, pp. 301-326.

An essay on Tadeusz Kroński in T. Kroński *Rozważania wokół Hegla* (Studies Around Hegel), Warsaw, 1960, pp. 493-499.

Der Mensch ohne Alternative: Von der Möglichkeit und Unmöglichkeit Marxist zu Sein, Munich, 1960; second ed., 1964. Contains German translations by Wanda Bronska-Pampuch of eleven of Kołakowski's essays, all of which are listed separately above:

(1) "Aktuelle und nichtaktuelle Begriffe des Marxismus"
(2) "Die Intellektuellen und die kommunistische Bewegung"
(3) "Verantwortung und Geschichte"
(4) "Der Sinn des Begriffes 'Linke'"
(5) "Wovon leben die Philosophen?"

(6) "Die Antisemiten"

(7) "Die Weltanschauung und das tägliche Leben"

(8) "Der Platonismus, die Empirie und die öffentliche Meinung"

(9) "Über die Richtigkeit der Maxime 'Der Zweck heiligt die Mittel"

(10) "Lob der Inkonsequenz"

(11) "Der Priester und der Narr: Das theologische Erbe in der heutigen Philosophie"

"Wielkie i małe kompleksy humanistów" (Major and Minor Complexes of the Humanists), *Kultura i Społeczeństwo*, No. 1-2 (1960), pp. 63-80.

"Porażka chrześcijańskiej integracji racjonalizmu: Sprawa Fryderyka van Leenhof" (A Setback to the Christian Integration of Rationalism: The Case of Frederick van Leenhof), *Studia Filozoficzne*, No. 2 (1961), pp. 31-78. (English and Russian abstracts, pp. 78-79.)

"Irracjonalizacja religii jako produkt racjonalizmu. Sprawa Jana Bredenburga" (The Irrationalization of Religion as a Product of Rationalism. The Case of Jan Bredenburg), *Studia Filozoficzne*, No. 2-3 (1960), pp. 193-237. (With English and Russian abstracts.)

"Demon i płeć" (The Demon and Sex), *Twórczość*, No. 2 (1961), pp. 93-108.

"Wejście i wyjście" (Entrance and Exit), an unpublished two-act play, produced in Warsaw in 1962. Part of the second act was published as: "Wielkie kazanie księdza Bernarda" (Father Bernard's Great Sermon), *Twórczość*, No. 10 (1961), pp. 8-16.

"Zakresowe i funkcjonalne rozumienie filozofii" (Philosophy Interpreted in Terms of Scope and of Function), *Kultura i Społeczeństwo*, No. 1 (1962), pp. 3-19.

"Cogito, materializm historyczny, i ekspresyjna interpretacja osobowości" (The *cogito*, Historical Materialism, and the Expressive Interpretation of the Individual Person), *Studia Socjologiczne*, No. 3 (1962), pp. 57-90.

Notatki o współczesnej kontrreformacji (Notes on the Contemporary Counter-Reformation), Warsaw, 1962.

"Husserl—filozofia doświadczenia rozumiejącego" (Husserl—A Philosophy of Interpretive Experience), in *Filozofia i socjologia XX wieku* (Twentieth-Century Philosophy and Sociology), Warsaw, 1962, pp. 103-124.

"U począków drugeij reformacji (Prawo i ewangelia)" (The Origins of the Second Reformation [The Law and the Gospels]), *Euhemer—Przegląd Religioznawczy*, No. 4 (1962), pp. 3-25.

"Etyka bez kodeksu" (Ethics without a Code), *Twórczość*, No. 7 (1962), pp. 64-86.

"Antykonfesjonalny nurt Mennonicki wobec religio rationalis" (The Anti-Confessional Tendency of the Mennonites vis-à-vis *religio rationalis*), in *Religie racjonalne: Studia z filozofii religii XV-XVII w.: Archiwum Historii Filozofii i Myśli Społecznej* (Rational Religion: Studies in the Philosophy of Religion of the Fifteenth to Seventeenth Century: Archive for the History of Philosophy and Social Thought), Vol. 9 (Warsaw, 1963), pp. 5-66. (German abstract, p. 67).

13 bajek z królestwa Lailonii dla dużych i małych (Thirteen Fables from the Kingdom of Lailonia for Grownups and Children), Warsaw, 1963.

"Trzy monologi" (Three Monologues), *Twórczość*, No. 4 (1963), pp. 7-21. (Imaginary soliloquies of Orpheus, Héloise, and Schopenhauer.)

Filozofski eseji (Philosophical Essays), Belgrade, 1964, with an introductory essay by Sveta Lukić. Serbo-Croatian translations by Svetozar Nikolić of the following eight essays (listed separately above):

(1) "The Priest and the Jester"
(2) "World-View and Everyday Life"
(3) "Ethics without a Code"
(4) "In Praise of Inconsistency"
(5) "Essence and Existence in the Concept of Freedom"
(6) "The *cogito*, Historical Materialism, and the Expressive Interpretation of the Individual Person"
(7) "Karl Marx and the Classical Definition of Truth"
(8) "Philosophy Interpreted in Terms of Scope and of Function"

Mivchar ma'amarim (A Selection of Essays), Merchaviah, 1964. Hebrew translations of the following twelve essays (listed separately above):

(1) "The Intellectuals and the Communist Movement"
(2) "Responsibility and History"
(3) "The Ideological Significance of the Concept 'Left'"
(4) "What do Philosophers Live by?"
(5) "World-View and Everyday Life"

(6) "Platonism, Empiricism, and Public Opinion"

(7) "On the Validity of the Maxim: The End Sanctifies the Means"

(8) "In Praise of Inconsistency"

(9) "The Priest and the Jester"

(10) "The Limits of Freedom" (ch. VI of Kołakowski's book on Spinoza)

(11) "Karl Marx and the Classical Definition of Truth"

(12) "Ethics without a Code"

Kołakowski has also written introductions to Polish editions of the following texts:

Uriel d'Acosta, *Exemplar humanae vitae*, 1960; Spinoza, *Ethics*, 1954, *Correspondence*, 1961; Pascal, *Provincial Letters*, 1963; Gassendi, *Logic*, 1964; Michelet, *La Sorcière*, 1961; Bergson, *Creative Evolution*, 1956.

INDEX

A NOTE ON THE CONTRIBUTORS

José Ferrater Mora was educated at the University of Barcelona. He has taught in Cuba and Chile and is at present Professor of Philosophy at Bryn Mawr College. He is the author of more than a dozen books in Spanish and English, including *Man at the Crossroads* (1957), *Philosophy Today: Conflicting Tendencies in Contemporary Thought* (1960), and the monumental *Diccionario de filosofía*, soon to be published in its fifth (revised) edition. His most recent work is *El ser y la muerte: Bosquejo de filosofía integracionista* (1962).

Max H. Fisch was educated at Butler and Cornell Universities. He taught at Western Reserve University from 1928 until, during World War II, he became curator of rare books and head of the history of medicine division of the Army Medical Library. Since 1946 he has been Professor of Philosophy at the University of Illinois. He was visiting research professor at the University of Naples, 1950-1951, and visiting professor at Keio University in Tokyo, 1958-1959. He was chairman of the board of officers of the American Philosophical Association, 1956-1958, after serving as president of its Western Division, 1955-1956. His publications have been chiefly in the history of science and philosophy. With T. G. Bergin he translated Vico's *Autobiography* and *New Science*. He has published numerous articles and reviews on American philosophy; with P. R. Anderson he published *Philosophy in America* (1939). He edited *Classic American Philosophers* (1951). He is currently engaged in writing a biography of Charles S. Peirce.

J. Glenn Gray was educated at Juniata College, the University of Pittsburgh, and Columbia. He has taught at Swarthmore, Haverford, and the University of Pennsylvania, and is at present Professor of Philosophy and Chairman of the Department at Colorado College. His books include *Hegel's Hellenic Ideal* (1941) and *The Warriors: Reflections on Men in Battle* (1959). He has published a number of articles on Heidegger's philosophy. He has spent two years in Germany, as a Fulbright Research Scholar (1954-1955) and a Guggenheim Fellow (1961-1962). While preparing his contribution to the present volume in the summer of 1963, he again interviewed Heidegger.

171

HENRY S. HARRIS was educated at Oxford, Northwestern, and the University of Illinois. He has taught at The Ohio State University and the University of Illinois and is at present Associate Professor of Philosophy at York University (Toronto). He has published a number of studies concerning modern Italian philosophy and is the author of a book on *The Social Philosophy of Giovanni Gentile* (1960) and a translation of Gentile's *Genesis and Structure of Society*.

EUGENE F. KAELIN was educated at the University of Missouri, Bordeaux (France), and Illinois. He has taught at the University of Missouri and is at present Associate Professor of Philosophy at the University of Wisconsin. He has been post-doctoral fellow from the University of Illinois at the University of Bordeaux (1954), and an ACLS post-doctoral fellow at the Institute for Studies in the Humanities, University of Wisconsin (1960). He spent the year 1964-1965 studying in France and Germany. In 1962 the University of Wisconsin Press published his *An Existentialist Aesthetic*.

GEORGE L. KLINE was educated at Boston University, Columbia College, and Columbia University. He has taught at Columbia, The University of Chicago, and Swarthmore College and is at present Associate Professor of Philosophy and Russian at Bryn Mawr College. He is the author of *Spinoza in Soviet Philosophy* (1952), translator of Zenkovsky's *History of Russian Philosophy* (1953), and editor of *Alfred North Whitehead: Essays on His Philosophy* (1963). He has published numerous articles on Russian philosophy and intellectual history and on Spinoza, Hegel, Marx, and Whitehead.